William Cubitt Cooke

Popular British Ballads

Ancient and Modern

William Cubitt Cooke

Popular British Ballads
Ancient and Modern

ISBN/EAN: 9783744674300

Printed in Europe, USA, Canada, Australia, Japan

Cover: Foto ©Thomas Meinert / pixelio.de

More available books at **www.hansebooks.com**

Popular British Ballads

THE BATTLE OF OTTERBOURNE.—*p.* 184.

POPULAR
BRITISH BALLADS

ANCIENT AND MODERN

CHOSEN BY
R BRIMLEY JOHNSON
ILLUSTRATED BY
W CVBITT COOKE

IN FOVR VOLVMES

VOL: 1

> I NEVER HEARD
> THE OLD SONG
> OF PERCY AND
> DOUGLAS, THAT
> I FOUND NOT
> MY HEART
> MOVED MORE
> THAN WITH A
> TRUMPET
>
> SIR PHILIP
> SIDNEY

LONDON ❧ J. M. DENT & CO. Aldine House
69 Great Eastern Street E.C.
PHILADELPHIA ❧ J. B. LIPPINCOTT COMPANY
MDCCCXCIV

Dedication

ĕ

Life is all sunshine, dear,
If you are here:
Loss cannot daunt me, sweet,
If we may meet.—
As you have smiled on all my hours of play,
Now take the tribute of my working-day.

Aug. 3, 1894.

CONTENTS
VOL. I

I. Melismata: Musicall Phansies, Fitting the Court, Cittie, and Countrey Humours. London, 1611.

[*Melismata*, No. 20.]

This ballad has retained its hold on the country people for many centuries, and is still known in some parts. I have received a version from a gentleman in Lincolnshire, which his father (born Dec. 1793) had heard as a boy from an old labouring man, who could not read and had learnt it "from his fore-elders." Here the "fallow doe" has become a "lady full of woe."—See also *The Twa Corbies.*

II. Wit Restored. 1658.

[*Wit Restored*, reprint *Facetiæ*, I. 293.]

Percy notices that this ballad was quoted in many old plays—viz., Beaumont and Fletcher's *Knight of the*

Burning Pestle, v. 3 ; *The Varietie*, a Comedy, Act iv.
(1649); and Sir William Davenant's *The Wits*,
Act iii. Prof. Child also suggests that some stanzas
in Beaumont and Fletcher's *Bonduca* (v. 2) and
Fletcher's *Monsieur Thomas* (iv. 11) may be parodies
or reminiscences of the same.

THE TWA SISTERS 8

[Jamieson-Brown MS., fol. 39.]

This is one of the very few old ballads which is
still known and sung in country neighbourhoods
though it is not sold by Mr Such.[1] It goes by a
variety of names—*e.g.*, *Binnorie*, *The Miller and the
King's Daughter*, *The Cruel Sister*, *The Miller's
Melody*, &c. Judge Hughes has a version—*The
Drowned Lady*—in his *Scouring of the White Horse*,
with a ludicrous ending, which he tells me was
learnt in his nursery ; "one or two of the verses
were patched by his father."

The refrain varies much in the different versions. In
the earliest printed copy (*Wit Restor'd*) it is—

> With a hie down down a down—a.

In Scott's *Minstrelsy*—

> Binnorie, O Binnorie,
> By the bonnie mill-dams of binnorie.

In Motherwell's manuscript (printed by Prof.
Child)—

> Hey with the gay and the grandeur O,
> At the bonnie bows o' London town;

or in another part of the MS.—

> Hech, hey my Nannie O,
> And the swans swim bonnie O.

In *Notes and Queries*, from Lancashire—

> Bow down, bow down, bow down,
> I'll be true to my love and my love'll be true to me.

[1] Of 123 Union Street, Borough. He keeps a good stock of the old broadsides,
probably the largest in England.

[*MS. Ashmole*, Bodleian Library; reprinted by Prof. Skeat in his *Specimens of English Literature*, 3rd edition, 1880, p. 67.]

In his interesting paper on *Chevy-Chase* (*Gentleman's Magazine*, April 1889) Prof. Hales pointed out that this ballad and *The Battle of Otterbourne*, though confounded from an early date, "are connected with different localities, are based upon different incidents, and represent different features in the old Border life."

The Hunting of the Cheviot probably does not relate to any particular historical event, though Percy's suggestion that it was partially founded on the battle of Piperden (1435 or 1436), "appears to be well worth consideration." Such hunting expeditions, in which a Percy defied the March law and crossed the border to the Douglas territory, were doubtless of common occurrence; and the geography of this ballad is so vague, its chronology is so confused, that we cannot expect to identify it. The old men, quoted in the ballad, who knew the ground well, and call it the Battle of Otterburn, are no authorities.

The later version of this ballad, generally known as *Chevy-Chase*, was probably produced in the seventeenth century.

[*Percy Folio*, I. 248.]

This is one of the ballads to which Percy did little. There is a Scotch version called *Glenkindie*.

[Percy's *Reliques*, 1767, III. 119.]

This ballad begins like *Lord Thomas aud Fair Annet*, and has the same catastrophe as *Lord Lovel*. It is probably "the old song" quoted in Fletcher's *Knight of the Burning Pestle*, Acts II. and III. "The elegant production of David Mallet, Esq."—viz., *Margaret's Ghost*, which purported to be founded on the stanzas quoted by Fletcher, and was regarded by Percy as "one of the most beautiful ballads in our own or any language,"—has since been proved a fraud. A refined (!) version of our ballad, dated 1711, with the title of *William and Margaret, an old Ballad*, has been discovered, which Mr Mallet evidently touched up and published as his own.

[Percy's *Reliques*, 1765, I. 53.]

This ballad is sometimes regarded as a part of *The Twa Brothers*, with which it has considerable affinities. Motherwell printed a Scotch Version in 4-line stanzas, the second line being alternately the refrains :—"Son Davie, son Davie," and "Mother lady, mother lady." I have entirely dropped the affectedly antiquated spelling adopted by Percy, which has only served to raise suspicions of the ballad's authenticity.

The Contents ≈ xvii

PAGE

YOUNG WATERS 82

[Percy's *Reliques*, 1765, II. 172.]

This ballad has been associated by different editors
with various historical events, but there is no con-
clusive evidence on the subject.

THE CHILDREN IN THE WOOD 84

[Percy's *Reliques*, 1765, III. 218.]

There is an old English play (1601) "of a young child
murthered in a wood by two ruffians, with the
consent of his uncle," which was derived from the
Italian, and may have given some hints to the
author of this ballad.

HUGH OF LINCOLN 91

[Jamieson's *Popular Ballads*, I. 151.]

The whole subject of the various legends and traditions
with which this ballad in its various forms has been
associated may be best studied in *The Athenæum*,
Dec. 15, 1849. It has many similarities with the
beautiful *Tale of the Prioress* in Chaucer. Jamieson
obtained his version from the recitation of Mrs
Brown. It was known to the labourers of Lincolnshire, and probably of other parts, in very recent
years.

SIR PATRICK SPENCE 94

[Percy's *Reliques*, 1765, I. 71.]

A deputation, that sailed out in 1290 to bring over
Princess Margaret, the Maid of Norway, as bride
to Edward I., has been described as the origin of
this ballad; but the name of Sir Patrick Spence is
not historical, and there is no need to assume that
the ballad was founded on real events.

b

the farm of Blackhouse, in Selkirkshire. "Seven
large stones, erected upon the neighbouring heights
of Blackhouse, are shown, as marking the spot
where the seven brethren were slain; and the
Douglas burn is averred to have been the stream at
which the lovers stooped to drink."

[Arnold's *Chronicle*, 1502. Reprinted by T. Wright, 1836.]

Matthew Prior composed an "elegant" and tiresome
poem called *Henry and Emma* on the model of this
ballad.

[*Percy Folio*, II. 227.]

There is in existence a fragment of a dramatic piece
founded on the ballad of *Guy of Gisborne* and dated
1475 or earlier. Ritson remarks that Guy of
Gisborne is named in William Dunbar's *Sir Thomas
Norray* "along with our hero [*i.e.* Robin Hood],
Adam Bell, and other worthies, it is conjectured of
a similar stamp, but whose merits have not, less
fortunately, come to the knowledge of posterity."

[*Percy Folio*, I. 235.]

This is one of the ballads in which Percy made
considerable alterations.

[*Cotton MS.* in British Museum.]

"This ballad is founded upon a real event which took
place in the North of Scotland, in the year 1571,
during the struggles between the party which held
out for the imprisoned Queen Mary, and that
which endeavoured to maintain the authority of

her infant son, James VI."   Edom o' Gordon was
Adam Gordon of Auchindown, deputy-lieutenant
for the queen, who was a bitter enemy to the
Forbes clan, and, under colour of the queen's
authority, "sent a party under one Captain Car
or Ker, to reduce the house of Towie, one of the
chief seats of the name of Forbes." Car executed
his commission after the fashion described in the
ballad, and Gordon, having never cashiered him,
was regarded as equally responsible for the out-
rage. In some versions of the ballad he is
represented as the principal actor himself.

[Scott's *Minstrelsy*, I. 345.]

In Professor Hale's paper on Chevy-Chase, already
referred to over that ballad, the history of the
Battle of Otterbourne is fully described. It is
an incident in the "raid" into English territory
which was undertaken "in revenge of the invasion
of Scotland by Richard II. in 1387." The small
division under the command of Douglas, with
which we are concerned, marched over the
Cheviots, pillaged Durham, and re-crossing the
Tyne, halted before Newcastle. "And then it
was, after some skirmishing, that, according to
the ballad, Douglas made a tryst to meet Percy at
Otterbourne." This Percy is Shakespeare's Hot-
spur. The longer and less poetical English
version, printed by Bp. Percy, describes the whole
battle with greater detail, but throws less fire
into the personal contest.

*VII. Ancient and Modern Scottish Songs, Heroic
Ballads, etc. By David Herd,* 2 *vols.* 1769
and 1776.

yard of Kirkconnell, "a romantic spot, almost
surrounded by the river Kirtle." One evening Bell
"appeared suddenly on the opposite bank, and
levelled his carebine at the breast of his rival.
Helen threw herself before her lover, received in
her bosom the bullet, and died in his arms."

A First Part, apparently an address by Fleming
or his rival to the lady, was also published by
Scott, but is so inferior that it is impossible to
believe it the work of the same hand.

Elegies on Helen have been written by Pinkerton
(*Select Scottish Ballads*, I. 109); Mayne (*Gentleman's
Magazine*, vol. 86, part ii., 64); Jamieson (*Popular
Ballads*, 1205); and Wordsworth's *Ellen Irvin* was
inspired by the same subject.

[Jamieson's *Popular Ballads*, I. 66.]

This ballad is sometimes known as *The Three Knights,
or Fine Flowers in the Valley.*
The refrain varies in the different versions.
In Herd's *Scottish Songs*—

> Fine flowers i' the valley
> The red, the green, and the yellow.

In Gilbert's *Ancient Christmas Carols*—

> With the high and the lily oh !
> As the rose was so sweetly blown.

[Jamieson's *Popular Ballads*, I. 176.]

Sometimes called *Lambert Linkin, Bold Rankin, Long
Lankyn, Lammikin,* &c.

[*Border Minstrelsy*, III. 263.]

Sometimes known as *Bothwell, Child Brenton, Lord
Dingwall, We were sisters, we were seven,* &c.

[Caw's *Museum*, p. 145.]

Jock o' the Side was, apparently, a nephew of the Laird
of Mangertoun (the chief of the clan of Armstrong)
who assisted the escape of the Earl of Westmoreland
after the Rising in the North, 1569, in which the
Earl of Northumberland also took part. Prof.
Child suggests that the ballad may be a free
version of Kinmont Willie's story. There was
an incomplete version in Percy's *Folio* which he
did not use.

[Ritson's *Ancient Songs and Ballads*, quoted in the editor's
"Dissertation."]

This charming fragment is one of the scraps of songs
occurring in W. Wager's *The longer thou livest the
more fool thou art*, 1575, and, in the opinion of Mr
Ebsworth, may be dated before 1568.

[Ritson's *Scottish Songs*, II. 35.]

This fragment is so superior to the complete ballad on
the same subject, that it must be left to itself.
The fire was an episode in a mortal feud between

LIST OF
ILLUSTRATIONS

List of Illustrations ≈ xxix

The
Preface

1. THE word "ballad" is admittedly of very wide significance. Meaning originally "a song intended as the accompaniment to a dance," it was afterwards applied to "a light simple song of any kind" with a leaning towards the sentimental or romantic; and, in its present use, is defined by Dr Murray as "a simple spirited poem in short stanzas, in which some popular story is graphically told." Passing over the obsolete sense of "a popular song specially celebrating or scurrilously attacking some person or institution," we may note that Dr Johnson calls a ballad "a song," and quotes a statement from Watts that it once "signified a solemn and sacred song as well as a trivial, when Solomon's

Song was called the 'The Ballad of Ballads,' but now it is applied to nothing but trifling verse."

Ballad-collectors, however, have never strictly regarded any one of these definitions, and to me their catholicity seems worthy of imitation. I have demanded no more of a ballad than that it should be a simple spirited narrative ; and, though excluding the pure lyrics and metrical romances found in Percy's *Reliques* or elsewhere, I have been guided in doubtful cases rather by intuition than by rule. I have included poems written in every variety of metre except blank verse, and even the latter may seem to be represented by Blake's *Fair Elinor.*

Moreover, this is a collection of poems, not of archæological specimens or verses on great historic events ; and the ballads have been chosen according to my judgment of their artistic merits.

2. Vols. I. and II. contain the best traditionary ballads of England and Scotland, with a small group of Peasant Ballads still sung in country

districts. Vols. III. and IV. contain selected modern experiments in the art of ballad-writing by English, Scotch, and Welsh poets, with a mixed group of Irish ballads; those on foreign or classical subjects being in each case excluded.

a. The text of the old ballads has been carefully prepared from the best authorities, and the spelling is modernised so far as can be done without injuring the rhythm or accentuation. Brief historical or explanatory notes are printed in the Table of Contents, and obsolete terms are explained in footnotes.

No attempt has been made to settle disputed dates of composition, but the ballads are arranged in groups according to the collection (*e.g.* Percy's *Reliques*, Scott's *Minstrelsy*, etc.) in which they were first included, and thus brought before the notice of the literary public. The groups are arranged according to the dates of publication of the collections.

b. For the Peasant Ballads one text is seldom more authoritative than another, and minor differences have to be settled by personal judgment. The versions here offered, have, in many cases, been prepared from those popular in different parts of England. They are believed to represent the most poetical form of the songs which were the favourites of the elder generation, and which are being now superseded by the shorter and more sensational effusions of the music-hall. They are arranged according to their subjects.

c. The modern ballads are arranged chronologically, according to the dates of birth of their authors, and are intended to be, so far as possible, representative of our best poets. Parodies and dialect poems have been purposely omitted, because they form classes by themselves and are essentially different in spirit from both the traditionary and the literary ballads. This restriction does not involve the omission of all poems with humorous subjects or treatment.

By calling these ballads " modern " I do not wish to imply that every one of them was written later than those in Vols. I. and II., since it is practically certain that some of the Peasant group

belong to this century. They are modern in the
sense of being literary productions by known
authors, which were offered to the public in a
printed form from the first.

d. Irish ballads, written in English, are comparatively modern, but they belong to the
traditionary manner and, whether the work
of ballad-mongers or of poets, need not be
separated from the few translations from the
Irish which have been thought suitable for this
collection. They too are arranged chronologically.

e. A similar group of Welsh ballads was
projected, but after a careful investigation of
the principal periodicals and collections, and
some correspondence with students of Welsh
literature, I have concluded that, for English
readers at least, there exist but few Welsh
ballads of any merit; and that the poetic genius
of the nation could not be fairly represented by
such a selection.

3. *a.* Every student of our old ballads owes
an immeasurable debt of gratitude to Professor

F. J. CHILD, whose monumental collections * have covered the entire field. I have naturally followed his guidance in the choice of texts and used his transcripts from manuscripts, having received his cordial permission to do so, in letters of kind advice and sympathy.

My thanks are also due to Dr Furnivall and Professor Hales for answers to questions and permission to follow their reprint of *The Percy Folio*; to Professor Skeat for the use of his transcript of *The Hunting of the Cheviot*; to Mr W. C. Hazlitt for a portion of an old copy of *Adam Bell, Clym of the Clough, and William Cloudeslè*; and to the Council of the Folk-lore Society for the version of the *Unquiet Grave* which appeared in their *Record*.

b. In the preparation of the Peasant group I have received great assistance from the Rev. S. BARING-GOULD, who has generously put at my disposal the results of his life-long studies in

---

* " English and Scottish Ballads," in 8 vols. (Houghton, Mifflin & Co.) ; " The English and Scottish Ballads "—in the course of publication—Parts i.-viii. having already appeared (Houghton, Mifflin & Co.).

this subject, given me advice and information at every turn, and allowed me the free use of all his own manuscript and printed material. Without his help and encouragement this part of the work could never have been completed.

My thanks are also due to numerous members of the Folk-lore Society, both in London and the provinces, among whom I would particularly mention Miss C. S. Burne, author of *Shropshire Folk-lore*, and Mrs Balfour of Northumberland.

I have received much assistance also from Miss Lucy E. Broadwood, who has united with Mr J. A. Fuller-Maitland and the Leadenhall Press, Ltd., in permitting me to reprint from her *English County Songs*.

For replies to various questions on these subjects I am indebted to Messrs A. T. Quiller-Couch, W. E. A. Axon, Edward Peacock, the Rev. J. C. Atkinson, Judge Hughes, Miss Field, and Miss G. Chanter. Messrs G. Bell & Sons have kindly allowed me to reprint " Sir Arthur

and charming Mollee " from their *Ancient Poems,
Ballads, and Songs of the Peasantry of England.*

c. For the use of copyright matter my thanks
are further due to Messrs Macmillan & Co.,
the publishers of Charles Kingsley, and Miss
Rossetti; to Messrs Smith, Elder & Co., of
Robert Browning; to Messrs Chatto & Windus,
of G. W. Thornbury; to Messrs Elis & Elvey,
of D. G. Rossetti; Messrs Ward, Lock &
Bowden, of Henry Kingsley; Messrs Kegan
Paul & Co., of Mrs Hamilton-King; Messrs
Messina & Co., Melbourne, of A. L. Gordon;
and Mr C. Baxter, the agent of Mr R. L.
Stevenson.

I am also indebted to Sir George Young, Bart.,
for information concerning W. M. Praed; to
Mr Sebastian Evans; Mrs W. B. Scott; Mrs
Dobell; Dr George MacDonald; Miss Jean
Ingelow and her publishers, Messrs Longmans,
Green & Co.; Mrs Isa Craig Knox; Mrs
Calverly; Dr Garnett; Mrs Cory and the
publisher of the late William Cory, Mr George
Allen; Mr A. C. Swinburne; Madame Darm-

steter; Miss Grant; Mr Ernest Rhys; Mr R. Buchanan; Mr John Davidson; Mr Rudyard Kipling and his publishers, Messrs Methuen & Co., and Messrs Thacker & Co.; and Miss G. Chanter.

Having found every endeavour vain to discover the address of the Misses Hawker, I have ventured to reprint *The Doom of St Madron*, by the late R. S. Hawker, without their permission, the publishers, Messrs Kegan Paul & Co., offering no objection so far as they are concerned. From the works of Tennyson, Mr Wm. Morris, and a few others, I should have made selections, had not the permission been, to my great regret, withheld.

d. In the preparation of the Irish group I have been very materially assisted by Mr ALFRED PERCIVAL GRAVES, who has advised my selection and given me the free use of all his own work; and by Mr DAVID J. O'DONOGHUE, author of the *Dictionary of the Poets and Poetry of Ireland*, who has devoted much time to supplying me with information of all kinds, and directing me to the work of comparatively unknown authors.

For the use of copyright matter I am also indebted to Mrs Allingham; to Professor E. F. Savage-Armstrong, for his own work, and that of his brother, the late Edward J. Armstrong; to Lady Ferguson; Miss Emily H. Hickey; Mr Michael Hogan; Mr Wm. Winter and Messrs C. Scribner & Sons, for a poem by Fitzjames O'Brien; Messrs Routledge & Sons for poems by S. Lover; to Mr T. D. Sullivan, M.P.; Mrs K. Tynan (Hinkson); Mr Aubrey de Vere and his publishers, Messrs Macmillan & Co.; Mr W. B. Yeats; and Dr Sigerson.

Finally, I have to thank Mr Theodore Watts and Mr Alfred H. Miles, editor of *The Poets and Poetry of the Century*, for information on certain questions of copyright.

R. BRIMLEY JOHNSON.

LLANDAFF HOUSE, CAMBRIDGE,
August 3rd, 1894.

ERRATA.

Page xviii,	line	14,	*for* "Bell,"	*read* "Bel."
"	"	"	15, " "Willyam,"	" "William."
"	3,	"	12, " "amonst,"	" "amongst."
"	4,	"	19, " "allthough,"	" "although."
"	12,	"	5, " "doughtè,"	" "doughty."
"	"	"	16, " "hillys,"	" "hills."
"	16,	"	5, " "Cristes,"	" "Christ's."
"	17,	"	5, " "yebent,"	" "ybent."
"	19,	"	21, " "cam,"	" "came."
"	22,	"	2, " "befor,"	" "before."
"	37,	"	13, " "bid,"	" "did."
"	40,	"	15, " "borne,"	" "born."
"	42,	"	7, " "froe,"	" "fro."
"	46,	"	22, " "bleede,"	" "bleed."
"	47,	"	27, " "shoot,"	" "shot."
"	64,	"	16, " "down,"	" "doun."
"	79,	"	12, " "no,"	" "nae."
"	80,	footnote,	" "die,"	" "are."

" His hounds they lie down at his feet,
So well they can their master keep.

A

me to the work of comparatively unknown

LLANDAFF HOUSE, CAMBRIDGE,
August 3rd, 1894.

The Three Ravens

THERE were three ravens sat on a tree,
  Downe, a downe, hay downe, hay downe,
There were three ravens sat on a tree,
  · With a downe,
There were three ravens sat on a tree,
They were as black as they might be,
  With a downe, derrie, derrie, derrie, downe,
    downe.

The one of them said to his mate,
" Where shall we our breakfast take ? "—

" Down in yonder green field,
There lies a knight slain under his shield.

" His hounds they lie down at his feet,
So well they can their master keep.

A

" His hawks they flie so eagerly,
There's no fowl dare him come nigh."

Down there comes a fallow doe,
As great with young as she might go.

She lift up his bloody head,
And kist his wounds that were so red.

She got him up upon her back,
And carried him to earthen lake.

She buried him before the prime,
She was dead herself ere even-song time.

God send every gentleman,
Such hawks, such hounds, and such a leman.

lake, grave.

Little
Musgrave
and
Lady
Barnard

As it fell one holy-day, *hay down*,
  As many be in the year,
When young men and maids together did go
  Their matins and mass to hear,

Little Musgrave came to the church door,
  The priest was at private mass ;
But he had more mind of the fair women,
  Then he had of our lady's grace.

The one of them was clad in green,
  Another was clad in pall ;
And then came in my lord Barnard's wife,
  The fairest amonst them all.

She cast an eye on little Musgrave,
　As bright as the summer sun,
And then bethought this little Musgrave,
　" This lady's heart have I won."

Quoth she, " I have loved thee, little Musgrave,
　Full long and many a day : "
" So have I loved you, fair lady,
　Yet never word durst I say."

" I have a bower at Bucklesfordbery,
　Full daintily it is dight ;
If thou wilt wend thither, thou little Musgrave,
　Thou's lig in mine arms all night."

Quoth he, " I thank ye, fair lady,
　This kindness thou showest to me ;
But whether it be to my weal or woe,
　This night I will lig with thee."

With that he heard a little tiny page,
　By his lady's coach-as he ran :
" Allthough I am my lady's footpage,
　Yet I am lord Barnard's man.

" My lord Barnard shall know of this,
　Whether I sink or swim : "
And ever where the bridges were broke,
　He laid him down to swim.

" Asleep, or wake ! thou lord Barnard,.
   As thou art a man of life ;
For little Musgrave is at Bucklesfordbery,
   Abed with thy own wedded wife."

" If this be true, thou little tiny page,
   This thing thou tellest to me,
Then all the land in Bucklesfordbery
   I freely will give to thee.

" But if it be a lie, thou little tiny page,
   This thing thou tellest to me,
On the highest tree in Bucklesfordbery.
   Then hangèd shalt thou be."

He called up his merry men all :—
   " Come saddle me my steed ;
This night must I to Bucklesfordbery,
   For I never had greater need."

And some of them whistl'd, and some of them
         sung,
   And some these words did say,
And ever when my lord Barnard's horn blew,
   " Away, Musgrave, away ! "

" Methinks I hear the thresel-cock,
   Methinks I hear the jay ;
Methinks I hear my Lord Barnard,—
   And I would I were away."

thresel-cock, thrush.

" Lie still, lie still, thou little Musgrave,
  And huggell me from the cold ;
'Tis nothing but a shephard's boy,
  A driving his sheep to the fold.

" Is not thy hawk upon a perch ?
  Thy steed eats oats and hay,
And thou a fair lady in thine arms,—
  And wouldst thou be away ? "

With that my lord Barnard came to the door,
  And lit a stone upon ;
He plucked out three silver keys,
  And he open'd the doors each one.

He lifted up the coverlet,
  He lifted up the sheet ;
" How now, how now, thou little Musgrave,
  ·Doest thou find my lady sweet ? "

" I find her sweet," quoth little Musgrave,
  " The more 'tis to my pain ;
I would gladly give three hundred pounds
  That I were on yonder plain."

" Arise, arise, thou little Musgrave,
  And put thy clothés on ;
It shall ne'er be said in my country,
  I have killed a naked man.

" I have two swords in one scabbard,
　　Full dear they cost my purse ;
And thou shalt have the best of them,
　　And I will have the worse."

The first stroke that little Musgrave stroke,
　　He hurt Lord Barnard sore ;
The next stroke that Lord Barnard stroke,
　　Little Musgrave ne'er struck more.

With that bespake this fair lady,
　　In bed whereas she lay ;
" Although thou'rt dead, thou little Musgrave,
　　Yet I for thee will pray ;

" And wish well to thy soul will I,
　　So long as I have life ;
So will I not for thee, Barnard,
　　Although I am thy wedded wife."

He cut her paps from off her breast,
　　Great pity it was to see,
That some drops of this lady's heart's blood
　　Ran trickling down her knee.

" Woe worth you, woe worth, my merry men all,
　　You were ne'er born for my good ;
Why did you not offer to stay my hand,
　　When ye saw me wax so wood !

" For I have slain the bravest sir knight
　　That ever rode on steed ;
So have I done the fairest lady
　　That ever did woman's deed.

" A grave, a grave," Lord Barnard cried,
　　To put these lovers in ;
But lay my lady on the upper hand,
　　For she came of the better kin."

　　　　　　　—≫≡-≡≪—

The Twa

Sisters

ě

THERE was twa sisters in a bow'r,
　　　　Edinburgh, Edinburgh,
There was twa sisters in a bow'r,
　　　　Stirling for aye,
There was twa sisters in a bow'r,
There came a knight to be their wooer,
　　　　Bonny Saint Johnston stands upon Tay.

He courted the eldest wi' glove an' ring,
But he loved the youngest above a' thing.

He courted the eldest wi' brooch an' knife,
But loved the youngest as his life ;

The eldest she was vexed sair,
An' much envied her sister fair ;

Into her bower she could not rest,
Wi' grief an' spite she almost brast.

Upon a morning fair an' clear
She cried upon her sister dear :

O sister come to yon sea-stran',
And see our father's ships come to lan'.

She's ta'en her by the milk-white han',
And led her down to yon sea-stran'.

The youngest stood upon a stane,
The eldest came an' threw her in ;

She took her by the middle sma',
An' dash'd her bonny back to the jaw ;

O sister, sister, take my han',
An I'se make you heir to a' my lan'.

O sister, sister, take my middle,
And ye's get my gold and my golden girdle.

jaw, wave.

O sister, sister, save my life,
And I swear I'se never be nae man's wife.

" Foul fa' the han' that I should take,
It twin'd me an' my wardle's make."

" Your cherry cheeks and yallow hair,
Gars me gae maiden for evermair."

. Sometimes she sank, an' sometimes she swam,
Till she cam down yon bonny mill dam ;

O out it came the miller's son,
An' saw the fair maid swimmin' in.

" O father, father, draw your dam !
Here's either a mermaid, or a swan."

The miller quickly drew the dam,
An' there he found a drown'd woman ;

twin'd, deprived.   *wardle's make*, life-mate.

You couldna see her yallow hair,
For gold and pearl that were sae rare ;

You couldna see her middle sma',
For golden girdle that was sae braw ;

Ye couldna see her fingers white
For golden rings that was sae gryte.

And by there came a harper fine,
That harped to the king at dine.

When he did look that lady upon,
He sigh'd and made a heavy moan ;

He's taen three locks o' her yallow hair,
And wi' them strung his harp sae fair.

The first tune he did play and sing
Was—" Farewell to my father the king."

The nexten tune that he played syne
Was—" Farewell to my mother the queen."

The lasten tune that he play'd then
Was—" Wae to my sister, fair Ellen ! "

gryte, great.

≋ The Hunting
≋ of the Cheviot

THE FIRST FIT.

THE Persè out of Northumberland,
  And a vow to God made he,
That he would hunt in the mountains
  Of Cheviot within days three,
In the magger of doughtè Douglas,
  And all that ever with him be.

The fattest harts in all Cheviot
  He said he would kill, and carry them away :
" By my faith," said the doughty Douglas again,
  " I will let that hunting if that I may."

Then the Persè out of Banborowe came,
  With him a mighty meany ;
With fifteen hundrith archers bold of blood and
    bone,
  They were chosen out of shires three.

This began on a Monday at morn,
  In Cheviot the hillys so he ;
The child may rue that is un-born,
  It was the more pity.

in the magger, in the maugre—*i.e.* in spite of.   *let*, hinder.
    meany, company.   *so he*, so high.

The drivers thorow the woodès went,
    For to raise the deer;
Bowmen byckarte upon the bent
    With their broad arrows clear.

Then the wyld thorow the woodès went,
    On every sydë shear;
Greyhounds thorow the grevis glent,
    For to kill their deer.

Thus began in Cheviot the hills abone,
    Early on a Monnyn day;
By that it drew to the hour of noon,
    A hundrith fat harts dead there lay.

They blew a mort upon the bent,
    They sembled on sydës shear;

byckarte, hurried.   *bent*, plain.   *wyld*, deer.   *shear*, at once.
grevis, groves.   *glent*, glanced.   *sembled shear*, assembled together.
    blew a mort, sounded a horn for the dead.

To the quarry then the Persè went,
  To see the brittling of the deer.

He said, " It was the Douglas promise
  This day to meet me here ;
But I wist he would fail, verament : "
  A great oath the Persè swear.

At the last a squire of Northumberland
  Looked at his hand full nigh ;
He was ware o' the doughty Douglas coming,
  With him a mighty meany ;

Both with spear, billè, and brand ;
  It was a mighty sight to see ;
Hardier men, both of heart nor hand,
  Were not in Christiantè.

·There were twenty hundrith spear-men good,
  Withowtè any fail ;
They were born along by the water o' Twyde,
  Ith' bounds of Tividale.

"Leave of the brittling of the deer," he said,
  " And to your bows look ye take good heed ;
For never sith ye were on your mothers born
  Had ye never so mickle need."

brittling, cutting up.   *ware*, aware.   *meany*, company.
          billè, battle-axe.   *sith*, since.

The doughty Douglas on a steed
He rode all his men beforne ;
His armour glittered as did a glede ;
A bolder bairn was never born.

" Tell me whose men ye are," he says,
" Or whose men that ye be :
Who gave you leave to hunt in this Cheviot chase,
In the spite of mine and me ? "

The first man that ever him an answer made,
It was the good lord Persè :
" We will not tell thee whose men we are," he
says,
" Nor whose men that we be ;
But we will hunt here in this chase,
In the spite of thine and of thee.

" The fattest harts in all Cheviot
We have killed, and cast to carry them a-way : "
" Be my troth," said the doughty Douglas again,
" Therefore the one of us shall die this day."

Then said the doughty Douglas
Unto the lord Persè :
" To kill all these guiltless men,
Alas, it were great pity !

glede, burning gold.   cast, intend.

" But, Persè, thou art a lord of land,
   I am an Earl called within my contrè ;
Let all our men upon a party stand,
   And do the battle of thee and of me."

" Now Cristes corpse on his crown," said
   the lord Persè,
  " Whosoever there-to says nay ;
By my troth, doughty Douglas," he says,
  " Thou shalt never see that day.

" Neither in England, Scotland, nor France,
   Nor for no man of a woman born,
But, and fortune be my chance,
   I dare meet him, one man for one."

Then bespake a squire of Northumberland,
  Richard Wytharyngton was him name ;
" It shall never be told in South-England,"
   he says,
  " To king Harry the fourth for shame.

" I wot you bin great lordes twa,
   I am a poor squire of land ;
I will never see my captain fight on a field,
   And stand myself, and lookè on,
But while I may my weapon wield,
   I will not [fail] both heart and hand."

That day, that day, that dreadfull day !
  The first fit here I find ;
And you will hear any more a' the hunting a' the
    Cheviot,
  Yet is there more behind.

THE SECOND FIT.

THE English men had their bows yebent,
  Their·hearts were good enough ;
The first of arrows that they shot off,
  Seven score spear-men they slough.

Yet bides the Earl Douglas upon the bent,
  A captain good enough,
And that was seenè verament,
  For he wrought home both woe and wouche.

The Douglas parted his hòst in three,
  Like a cheffe chieftan of pride,
With sure spears of mighty trèe,
  They come in on every side :

Through our English archery
  Gave many a wound full wide ;
Many a doughty they gard to die,
  Which gained them no pride.

find, end.   *And*, if.   *slough*, slew.   *wouche*, injury.
                tree, wood.   *gard*, made.

The English men let their bows be,
    And pulled out brands that were bright ;
It was a heavy sight to see
    Bright swords on basnets light.

Thorow rich mail and maniple,
    Many sterne the stroke down straight ;
Many a freyke that was full free,
    There under foot did light.

basnets, helmets.   *light*, alight.
sterne, drove.   *freyke*, warrior.   *free*, noble.

At last the Douglas and the Persè met,
  Like to captains of might and of main ;
They swept together till they both swat,
  With swords that were of fine myllàn.

These worthè freykes for to fight,
  There-to they were full fain,
Till the blood out of their basnets sprent,
  As ever did hail or rain.

" Yield thee, Persè," said the Douglas,
  " And i' faith I shall thee bring
Where thou shalt have an earl's wages
  Of Jamy our Scottish king.

" Thou shalt have thy ransom free,
  I hight thee here this thing,
For the manfullest man yet art thou,
  , That ever I conquered in field fighting."

" Nay," said the lord Persè,
  " I told it thee beforne,
That I would never yielded be
  To no man of a woman born."

With that there cam an arrow hastely,
  Forth of a mighty wane ;
It hath striken the earl Douglas
  In at the breast bane.

myllan, steel. *sprent*, spurted. *hight*, promise. *wane*, crowd (?)

Thorow liver and lungs, baith
  The sharp arrow is gane,
That never after in all his life-days,
  He spake mo words but ane :
That was, " Fight ye, my merry men, whiles
    ye may,
  For my life-days ben gane."

The Persè leaned on his brand,
  And saw the Douglas dee ;
He took the dead man by the hand,
  And said, " Woe is me for thee !

" To have saved thy life, I would have parted
    with
  My landes for years three,
For a better man, of heart nor of hand,
  Was not in all the north contrè."

Of all that see a Scottish knight,
  Was called Sir Hew the Monggombyrry ;
He saw the Douglas to the death was dight,
  He spended a spear, a trusty tree :—

He rode upon a courser
  Through a hundrith archery :
He never stinted, nor never blane,
  Till he came to the good lord Persè.

dight, disposed of.   *spended*, grasped.   *blane*, stopped.

He set upon the lord Persè
   A dint that was full sore ;
With a sure spear of a mighty tree
   Clean thorow the body he the Persè bare,

A'the tother side that a man might see
   A large cloth yard and mair :
Two better captains were not in Christiantè,
   Than that day slain were there.

An archer of Northumberland
   Sae slain was the lord Persè ;
He bare a bend-bow in his hand,
   Was made of trusty tree.

An arrow, that a cloth yard was lang,
   To th' hard steel haled he ;
A dint that was both sad and sore,
   He set on Sir Hewe the Monggomberry.

The dint it was both sad and sore,
   That he of Monggomberry set ;
The swan-feathers, that his arrow bore,
   With his heart-blood they were wet.

There was never a freyke one foot would flee,
   But still in stour did stand,
Hewing on each other, while they might dree,
   With many a baleful brand.

bend-bow, bent bow.   *freyke*, warrior.   *stour*, fight.
dree, endure.

This battle began in Cheviot
　An hour befor the noon,
And when even-song bell was rang,
　The battle was not half done.

They took . . . on eithar hand
　By the light of the moon ;
Many had no strength for to stand,
　In Cheviot the hills aboun.

Of fifteen hundrith archers of England
　Went away but seventy and three ;
Of twenty hundrith spear-men of Scotland,
　But even five and fifty :

But all were slain Cheviot within ;
　They had no strength to stand on high ;
The child may rue that is unborn,
　˙ It was the more pity.

There was slain with the lord Persè,
　Sir John of Agerstone,
Sir Roger, the hind Hartly,
　Sir William, the bold Hearone.

Sir Jorg, the worthè Loumle,
　A knight of great renown,
Sir Raff, the rich Rugbè,
　With dints were beaten down.

For Wetharryngton my heart was woe,
   That ever he slain should be ;
For when both his legs were hewn in two,
   Yet he kneeled and fought on his knee.

There was slain with the doughty Douglas,
   Sir Hew the Monggomberry,
Sir Davy Lydale, that worthy was,
   His sister's son was he :

Sir Charls o' Murrè in that place,
   That never a foot would flee ;
Sir Hew Maxwell, a lord he was,
   With the Douglas did he dee.

So on the morrow they made them biers
   Of birch and hazel so gray ;
Many widows with weepng tears
   Came to fetch their makes away.

Tivydale may carp of care,
   Northumberland may make great moan,
For two such captains as slain were there,
   On the March-party shall never be none.

Word is commen to Eddenburrow,
   To Jamy the Scottish king,
That doughty Douglas, lieu-tenant of the
    Merches
   He lay slain Cheviot with-in.

makes, husband.   *carp*, talk.

His handes did he weal and wring,
   He said, " Alas, and woe is me ! "
Such an other captain Scotland within,
   He said, i-faith should never be.

Word is commen to lovely London,
   Till the fourth Harry our king,
That Lord Persè, lieu-tenant of the Marches
   He lay slain Cheviot within.

" God have mercy on his soul," said king
     Harry,
   " Good lord, if thy will it be !
I have a hundrith captains in England," he
     said,
   " As good as ever was he :
But Persè, and I brook my life,
   Thy death well quit shall be."

As our noble king made his a-vow,
   Like a noble prince of renown,
For the death of the lord Persè
   He did the battle of Hombyll-down :

Where six and thirty Scottish knights
   On a day were beaten down :
Glendale glittered on their armour bright,
   Over castle, tower, and town.

    weal, wring (?).   *brook*, preserve.   *quit*, requited.

This was the Hunting of the Cheviot ;
  That tear began this spurn :
Old men that knowen the ground well enough,
  Call it the battle of Otterburn.

At Otterburn began this spurn
  Upon a Monnyn day :
There was the doughty Douglas slain,
  The Persè never went away.

There was never a time on the March-partys
  Sen the Douglas and the Persè met,
But it was marvel, and the red blude ran not,
  As the rain does in the street.

Jesu Christ our balës bete,
  And to the bliss us bring !
Thus was the Hunting of the Cheviot :
  God send us all good ending !

tear, injury (?).   *spurn*, retaliation.   *sen*, when.
balës bete, sufferings better.

The

Blind

Beggar's

Daughter

of

Bednall

Green

ĕ

This song's of a beggar who long lost his sight,
And had a fair daughter, most pleasant and
    bright ;
And many a gallant brave suitor had she,
And none was so comely as pretty Bessee.

And though she was of complexion most fair,
Yet seeing she was but a beggar his heir,
Of ancient housekeepers despised was she,
Whose sons came as suitors to pretty Bessee.

Wherefore in great sorrow fair Bessee did say,
" Good father and mother, let me now go away,
To seek out my fortune, whatever it be ; "
This suit then was granted to pretty Bessee.

This Bessee, that was of a beauty most bright,
They clad in gray russet, and late in the night
From father and mother alone parted she,
Who sighed and sobbed for pretty Bessee.

She went till she came to Stratford-at-Bow,
Then she knew not whither or which way to go ;
With tears she lamented her sad destiny,
So sad and so heavy was pretty Bessee.

She kept on her journey until it was day,
And went unto Rumford along the highway ;
And at the King's Arms entertained was she,
So fair and well-favoured was pretty Bessee.

She had not been there one month at an end,
But master and mistress and all was her friend ;
And every brave gallant that once did her see
Was straightway in love with pretty Bessee.

Great gifts they did send her of silver and gold,
And in their songs daily her love they extoll'd ;
Her beauty was blazed in every degree,
So fair and so comely was pretty Bessee.

The young men of Rumford in her had their joy ;
She shewed herself courteous, but never too coy,
And at their commandment still she would be,
So fair and so comely was pretty Bessee.

Four suitors at once unto her did go,
They craved her favour, but still she said no ;
" I would not have gentlemen marry with me,"—
Yet ever they honoured pretty Bessee.

Now one of them was a gallant young knight,
And he came unto her disguised in the night ;
The second, a gentleman of high degree,
Who wooed and sued for pretty Bessee.

A merchant of London, whose wealth was not
    small,
Was then the third suitor, and proper withal ;
Her master's own son the fourth man must be,
Who swore he would die for pretty Bessee.

" If that thou wilt marry with me," quoth the
    knight,
" I'll make thee a lady with joy and delight ;
My heart is enthralled in thy fair beauty,
Then grant me thy favour, my pretty Bessee."

The gentleman said, " Come marry with me,
In silks and in velvets my Bessee shall be ;
My heart lies distracted, oh hear me ! " quoth he,
" And grant me thy love, my dear pretty Bessee."

" Let me be thy husband," the merchant did say,
" Thou shalt live in London most gallant and gay ;
My ships shall bring home rich jewels for thee,
And I will for ever love pretty Bessee."

Then Bessee she sighed, and thus she did say ;
" My father and mother I mean to obey ;
First get their goodwill, and be faithful to me,
And you shall enjoy your dear pretty Bessee."

To every one of them that answer she made ;
Therefore unto her they joyfully said,
" This thing to fulfill we all now agree ;
But where dwells thy father, my pretty Bessee ? "

" My father," quoth she, " is soon to be seen ;
The silly blind beggar of Bednall Green,
That daily sits begging for charity,
He is the kind father of pretty Bessee.

" His marks and his token are knowen full well ;
He always is led by a dog and a bell ;
A poor silly old man, God knoweth, is he,
Yet he is the true father of pretty Bessee."

" Nay, nay," quoth the merchant, " thou art not
      for me ; "
" She," quoth the innholder, " my wife shall not
      be ; "
" I loathe," said the gentleman, " a beggar's
      degree,
Therefore, now farewell, my pretty Bessee."

"Why then," quoth the knight, "hap better or
    worse,
I weigh not true love by the weight of the purse,
And beauty is beauty in every degree ;
Then welcome to me, my dear pretty Bessee.

"With thee to thy father forthwith I will go."
"Nay, forbear," quoth his kinsman, "it must
    not be so :
A poor beggar's daughter a lady sha'nt be ;
Then take thy adieu of thy pretty Bessee."

As soon then as it was break of the day,
The knight had from Rumford stole Bessee
    away ;
The young men of Rumford, so sick as may be,
Rode after to fetch again pretty Bessee.

As swift as the wind to ride they were seen,
Until they came near unto Bednall Green,
And as the knight lighted most courteously,
They fought against him for pretty Bessee.

But rescue came presently over the plain,
Or else the knight there for his love had been
    slain ;
The fray being ended, they straightway did see
His kinsman come railing at pretty Bessee.

Then bespoke the Blind Beggar, " Altho' I be
    poor,
Rail not against my child at my own door ;
Though she be not decked in velvet and pearl,
Yet I will drop angels with thee for my girl ;

" And then if my gold should better her birth,
And equal the gold you lay on the earth,
Then neither rail you, nor grudge you to see
The Blind Beggar's daughter a lady to be.

" But first, I will hear, and have it well known,
The gold that you drop it shall be all you own ; "
" With that," they replied, " contented we be ; "
" Then here's," quoth the beggar, " for pretty
    Bessee."

With that an angel he dropped on the ground,
And dropped, in angels, full three thousand
    pound ;
And oftentimes it proved most plain,
For the gentleman's one, the beggar dropped
    twain.

So that the whole place wherein they did sit
With gold was covered every whit ;
The gentleman having dropt all his store,
Said, " Beggar, your hand hold, for I have no
    more.

"Thou hast fulfilled thy promise aright ;"
"Then marry my girl," quoth he to the knight ;
"And then," quoth he, "I will throw you
    down,
An hundred pound more to buy her a gown."

The gentlemen all, who his treasure had seen,
Admired the Beggar of Bednall Green.
And those that had been her suitors before,
Their tender flesh for anger they tore.

Thus was the fair Bessee matched to a knight,
And made a lady in others' despite :
A fairer lady there never was seen
Than the Blind Beggar's daughter of Bednall
    Green.

But of her sumptuous marriage and feast,
And what fine lords and ladies there prest,
The second part shall set forth to your sight,
With marvellous pleasure, and wished for delight.

PART II.

Of a blind beggar's daughter so bright,
That late was betrothed to a young knight,
All the whole discourse thereof you did see,
But now comes the wedding of pretty Bessee.

It was in a gallant palace most brave,
Adorned with all the cost they could have,
This wedding it was kept most sumptuously,
And all for the love of pretty Bessee.

And all kind of dainties and delicates sweet
Was brought to their banquet, as it was thought
    meet ;
Partridge, and plover, and venison most free,
Against the brave wedding of pretty Bessee.

The wedding thro' England was spread by report,
So that a great number thereto did resort,
Of nobles and gentles of every degree,
And all for the fame of pretty Bessee.

To church then away went this gallant young
    knight,
His bride followed after, an angel most bright,
With troops of ladies, the like was ne'er seen,
As went with sweet Bessee of Bednall Green.

This wedding being solemnized then,
With music performed by skilfullest men,
The nobles and gentles sat down at that tide,
Each one beholding the beautiful bride.

But after the sumptuous dinner was done,
To talk and to reason a number begun,
And of the Blind Beggar's daughter most bright,
And what with his daughter he gave to the knight.

c

Then spoke the nobles, " Much marvel have we
This jolly blind beggar we cannot yet see!"
" My lords," quoth the bride, " my father so base
Is loathe with his presence these states to
　　disgrace."

" The praise of a woman in question to bring,
Before her own face, is a flattering thing ;
But we think thy father's baseness," quoth they,
" Might by thy beauty be clean put away."

They no sooner this pleasant word spoke,
But in comes the beggar in a silken cloak,
A velvet cap and a feather had he,
And now a musician, forsooth, he would be.

And being led in, from catching of harm,
He had a dainty lute under his arm ;
Said, " Please you to hear any music of me,
A song I will give you of pretty Bessee."

With that his lute he twanged straightway,
And thereon began most sweetly to play,
And after a lesson was played two or three,
He strained out this song most delicately :—

　　" *A beggar's daughter did dwell on a green,*
　　Who for her beauty might well be a queen,
　　A blithe bonny lass, and dainty was she,
　　And many one called her pretty Bessee.

" Her father he had no goods nor no lands,
But begged for a penny all day with his hands,
And yet for her marriage gave thousands three,
Yet still he hath somewhat for pretty Bessee.

" And here if any one do her disdain,
Her father is ready with might and with main,
To prove she is come of noble degree,
Therefore let none flout at my pretty Bessee."

With that the lords and the company round
With a hearty laughter were ready to swound ;
At last said the lords, " Full well we may see,
The bride and the bridegroom's beholden to thee."

With that the fair bride all blushing did rise,
With crystal water all in her bright eyes ;
" Pardon my father, brave nobles," quoth she,
" That through blind affection thus doats upon
    me."

" If this be thy father," the nobles did say,
" Well may he be proud of this happy day,
Yet by his countenance well may we see,
His birth with his fortune could never agree.

" And therefore, blind beggar, we pray thee
    bewray,
And look that the truth to us thou dost say,
Thy birth and thy parentage what it may be,
E'en for the love thou bearest to pretty Bessee."

"Then give me leave, ye gentles each one,
A song more to sing and then I'll begone;
And if that I do not win good report,
Then do not give me one groat for my sport : —

 "*When first our king his fame did advance,*
 And sought his title in delicate France,
 In many places great perils past he,
 But then was not born my pretty Bessee.

 "*And at those wars went over to fight,*
 Many a brave duke, a lord, and a knight,
 And with them young Monford of courage so free,
 But then was not born my pretty Bessee.

 "*And there did young Monford with a blow on*
     the face
 Lose both his eyes in a very short space;
 His life had been gone away with his sight,
 Had not a young woman gone forth in the night.

 "*Among the slain men, her fancy did move*
 To search and to seek for her own true love,
 Who seeing young Monford there gasping to die,
 She saved his life through her charity.

 "*And then all our victuals in beggars' attire,*
 At the hands of good people we then did require;
 At last into England, as now it is seen,
 We came, and remained in Bednall Green.

" *And thus we have lived in Fortune's despite,*
Though poor, yet contented, with humble delight,
And in my old years, a comfort to me,
God sent me a daughter called pretty Bessee.

" *And thus, ye nobles, my song I do end,*
Hoping by the same no man to offend ;
Full forty long winters thus I have been,
A silly blind beggar of Bednall Green.

Now when the company every one
Did hear the strange tale he told in his song,
They were amazed, as well as they might be,
Both at the blind beggar and pretty Bessee

With that the fair bride they all bid embrace,
Saying, " You are come of an honourable race ;
Thy father likewise is of high degree,
And thou art right worthy a lady to be."

Thus was the feast ended with joy and delight ;
A happy bridegroom was made the young
    knight,
Who lived in great joy and felicity,
With his fair lady, dear pretty Bessee.

Sir
Andrew
Barton

THE FIRST PART

As it befell in midsummer time,
  When birds sing sweetly on every tree,
Our noble King, King Henry the eighth,
  Over the river of Thames past he.
He was no sooner over the river,
  Down in a forest to take the air,
But eighty merchants of London city
  Came kneeling before King Henry there.

"O ye are welcome, rich merchànts,
  [Good sailors, welcome unto me!]"
They swore by the rood, they were sailors good,
  But rich merchànts they could not be.
"To France nor Flanders dare we not pass,
  Nor Bordeaux voyage we dare not fare;
And all for a false robber that lies on the seas,
  Who robs us of our merchant's ware."

King Henry was stout, and he turned him about,
　And swore by the Lord that was mickle of
　　might,
"I thought he had not been in the world
　　throughout,
That durst have wrought England such unright."
But ever they sighed, and said, "Alas!"
　Unto King Harry this answer again;
"He is a proud Scot, that will rob us all,
　If we were twenty ships, and he but one."

The king lookt over his left shoulder,
　Amongst his lords and barons so free;
"Have I never lord in all my realm,
　Will fetch yond traitor unto me?"
"Yes, that dare I," says my Lord Charles Howard;
　Near to the king whereas he did stand;
"If that your grace will give me leave,
　Myself will be the only man."

"Thou shalt have six hundred men," saith our
　　king;
　"And choose them out of my realm so free;
Besides mariners, and boys,
　To guide the great ship on the sea."
"I'll go speak with Sir Andrew," says Charles,
　　my lord Howard;
　"Upon the sea, if he be there,
I will bring him and his ship to shore.
　Or before my prince I will never come near."

The first of all my lord did call,
   A noble gunner he was one,
This man was threescore years and ten ;
   And Peter Simon was his name.
"Peter," says he, "I must sail to the sea,
   To seek out an enemy ; God be my speed!
Before all others I have chosen thee,
   Of a hundred gunners thou'st be my head."

"My lord," says he, "if you have chosen me
   Of a hundred gunners to be the head,
Hang me at your main-mast tree,
   If I miss my mark past three pence bread."
The next of all my lord he did call,
   A noble bowman he was one ;
In Yorkshire was this gentleman borne,
   And William Horsley was his name.

"Horsley," says he, "I must sail to the sea,
   To seek out an enemy ; God be my speed!
Before all others I have chosen thee ;
   Of a hundred bowmen thou'st be my head."
"My lord," says he, "if you have chosen me
   Of a hundred bowmen to be the head,
Hang me at your main-mast tree,
   If I miss my mark past twelve pence bread."

With pikes, and guns, and bowmen bold,
   This noble Howard is gone to the sea ;

bread, breadth.

On the day before mid-summer even,
   And out at Thames mouth sailed they.
They had not sailed days three,
   Upon their journey they took in hand,
But there they met with a noble ship,
   And stoutly made it both stay and stand.

"Thou must tell me thy name," says Charles,
     my lord Howard,
   "Or who thou art, or from whence thou came,
Yea, and where thy dwelling is,
   To whom and where thy ship does belong."
"My name," says he, "is Henry Hunt,
   With a pure heart, and a penitent mind;
I and my ship they do belong
   Unto the Newcastle that stands upon Tyne."

"Now thou must tell me, Harry Hunt,
   As thou hast sailed by day and by night,
Hast thou not heard of a stout robber;
   Men calls him Sir Andrew Barton, knight?"
But ever he sighed, and said, "Alas!
   Full well, my lord, I know that wight;
He robbed me of my merchant's ware,
   And I was his prisoner but yesternight.

"As I was sailing upon the sea,
   And [a] Bordeaux voyage as I did fare,
He clasped me to his hatch-board,
   And robbed me of all my merchant ware.

And I am a man, both poor and bare,
　　And every man will have his own of me,
And I am bound towards London to fare,
　　To complain to my prince Henry."

"That shall not need," says my Lord Howard;
　　"If thou canst let me this robber see,
For every penny he has taken thee froe
　　Thou shalt be rewarded a shilling," quoth he.
"Now God forefend," says Henry Hunt,
　　"My lord, you should work so far amiss!
God keep you out of that traitor's hands!
　　For you wot full little what a man he is.

"He is brass within, and steel without,
　　And beams he bears in his topcastle strong;
His ship hath ordinance clean round about,
　　Besides, my lord, he is very well manned.
He hath a pinnace, is dearly dight,
　　·St. Andrew's cross, that is his guide;
His pinnace bears ninescore men and more,
　　Besides fifteen canons on every side.

"If you were twenty ships, and he but one,
　　Either in hatchboard or in hall,
He would overcome you every one,
　　And if his beams they do down fall."
"This is cold comfort," says my lord Howard,
　　"To welcome a stranger thus to the sea:
I'll bring him and his ship to shore,
　　Or else into Scotland he shall carry me."

" Then you must get a noble gunner, my lord,
   That can set well with his eye,
And sink his pinnace into the sea,
   And soon then overcome will he be.
And when that you have done this,
   If you chance Sir Andrew for to board,
Let no man to his topcastle go
   And I will give you a glass, my lord.

" And then you need to fear no Scot,
   Whether you sail by day or by night ;
And to-morrow by seven of the clock,
   You shall meet with Sir Andrew Barton, knight.
I was his prisoner but yesternight,
   And he hath taken me sworn," quoth he ;
" I trust my L[ord] God will me forgive
   And if that oath then broken be."

" You must lend me six pieces, my lord," quoth he,
   " Into my ship, to sail the sea,
And to-morrow by nine of the clock
   Your Honour again then will I see."

THE SECOND PART.

AND the hatch-board where Sir Andrew lay
   Is hatched with gold dearly dight :
" Now by my faith," says Charles, my lord
     Howard,
   " Then yonder Scot is a worthy wight.

Take in your ancients, and your standards,
  Yea that no man shall them see ;
And put me forth a white willow wand,
  As merchants use to sail the sea."
But they stirred neither top nor mast [1] ;
  But Sir Andrew they passed by ;
" What English are yonder," said Sir Andrew,
  " That can so little courtesy ?

" I have been admiral over the sea
  More than these years three,
There is never an English dog nor Portingall
  Can pass this way without leave of me.
But now yonder pedlars they are past :
  Which is no little grief to me :
Fetch them back," says Sir Andrew Barton,
    " They all shall hang at my main-mast
      tree."

With that the pinnace it shot off ;
  That my Lord Howard might it well ken ;
It stroke down my lord's fore-mast,
  And killed fourteen of my lord his men.
" Come hither, Simon," says my lord Howard,
  " Look that thy words be true thou said ;
I'll hang thee at my main-mast tree,
    If thou miss thy mark past twelve pence
      bread."

---

[1] *i.e.* did not salute.

Simon was old, but his heart it was bold ;
   He took down a piece and laid it full low,
He put in chain yards nine,
   Besides other great shot less and more,
With that he let his gun-shot go ;
   So well he settled it with his eye,
The first sight that Sir Andrew saw,
   He see his pinnace sunk in the sea.

When he saw his pinnace sunk,
   Lord, in his heart he was not well !
" Cut my ropes ! it is time to be gone !
   I'll fetch yond pedlars back mysel'."
When my lord Howard saw Sir Andrew loose,
   Lord ! in his heart that he was fain ;
" Strike on your drums, spread out your
         ancients,
   Sound out your trumpets, sound out amain."

" Fight on, my men," says Sir Andrew Barton,
   " Weet, howsoever this gear will sway ;
It is my lord admiral of Englànd,
   Is come to seek me on the sea."
Simon had a son, with shot of a gun—
   Well Sir Andrew might it ken ;—
He shot it in at a privy place,
   And killed sixty more of Sir Andrew's men.

ancients, ensigns.   *weet*, know.
         gear, business or affair.

Harry Hunt came in at the other side ;
   And at Sir Andrew he shot then ;
He drove down his fore-mast tree,
   And killed eighty more of Sir Andrew's
      men.
" I have done a good turn," says Harry Hunt ;
   " Sir Andrew is not our king's friend ;
He hoped to have undone me yesternight,
   But I hope I have quit him well in the end."

" Ever alas ! " said Sir Andrew Barton,
   " What should a man either think or say ?
Yonder false thief is my strongest enemy,
   Who was my prisoner but yesterday.
Come hither to me, thou Gordon good,
   And be thou ready at my call,
And I will give thee three hundred pound,
   If thou wilt let my beams down fall."

With that he swarved the main-mast tree,
   So did he it with might and main ;
Horsley, with a bearing arrow,
   Stroke the Gordon through the brain ;
And he fell into the hatches again,
   And sore of this wound that he did bleede :
Then word went through Sir Andrew's men,
   That the Gordon he was dead.

swarved, sawed (?).

" Come hither to me, James Hamilton,
    Thou art my sister's son, I have no more ;
I will give [thee] six hundred pound
    If thou wilt let my beams down fall.
With that he swarved the main-mast tree,
    So did he it with might and main ;
Horsley, with another broad arrow,
    Strake the yeoman through the brain.

That he fell down to the hatches again,
    Sore of his wound that he did bleed :
Covetousness gets no gain,
    It is very true, as the Welshman said.
But when he saw his sister's son slain,
    Lord ! in his heart he was not well :
" Go fetch me down my armour of proof,
    For I will to the topcastle mysel'.

" Go fetch me down my armour of proof,
    For it is gilded with gold so clear ;
God be with my brother, John of Barton !
    Amongst the Portingalls he did it wear.
But when he had his armour of proof,
    And on his body he had it on,
Every man that looked at him,
    Said, gun nor arrow he need fear none."

" Come hither, Horsley," says my lord Howard,
    " And look your shaft that it go right ;
Shoot a good shoot in the time of need,
    And for thy shooting thou'st be made a knight."

" I'll do my best," says Horsley then,
  " Your honour shall see, before I go ;
If I should be hanged at your main-mast,
  I have in my ship but arrows two."

But at Sir Andrew he shot then,
  He made sure to hit his mark ;
Under the spole of his right arm
  He smote Sir Andrew quite through the heart.
Yet from the tree he would not start,
  But he clinged to it with might and main,
Under the collar then of his jack
  He stroke Sir Andrew thorough the brain.

" Fight on, my men," says Sir Andrew Barton,
  " I am hurt, but I am not slain ;
I'll lay me down and bleed awhile,
  And then I'll rise and fight again.
Fight on, my men," says Sir Andrew Barton,
  These English dogs they bite so low ;
Fight on for Scotland and St. Andrew,
  Till you hear my whistle blow."

But when they could not hear his whistle blow,
  Says Harry Hunt, " I'll lay my head
You may board yonder noble ship, my lord,
  For I know Sir Andrew he is dead."
With that they boarded this noble ship,
  So did they it with might and main ;
They found eighteen score Scots alive,
  Besides the rest were maimed and slain.

My Lord Howard took a sword in his hand,
  And smote off Sir Andrew's head ;
The Scots stood by did weep and mourn,
  But never a word durst speak or say.
He caused his body to be taken down
  And over the hatchboard cast into the sea,
And about his middle three hundred crowns :
  " Wheresoever thou lands, it will bury thee."

With his head they sailed into England again,
  With right good will, and force and main ;
And the day before new year's even
  Into Thames mouth they came again.

My Lord Howard wrote to King Henry's grace,
　With all the news he could him bring ;
" Such a new year's gift I have brought to your
　　grace
　As never did subject to any king.

" For merchandise and manhood,
　The like is not to be found ;
The sight of these would do you good,
　For you have not the like in your English
　　ground."
But when he heard tell that they were come
　Full royally he welcomed them home :
Sir Andrew's ship was the King's new year's
　　gift ;
　A braver ship you never saw none.

Now hath our king Saint Andrew's ship,
　Beset with pearls and precious stones ;
Now hath England two ships of war,
　Two ships of war, before but one.
" Who holp to this ? " says King Henry,
　" That I may reward him for his pain."
" Harry Hunt, and Peter Simon,
　William Horsley, and I the same.

" Harry Hunt shall have his whistle and chain,
　And all his jewels, whatsoever-they be,
And other rich gifts that I will not name,
　For his good service he hath done me.

Horsley, right thou'st be a knight,
   Lands and livings thou shalt have store ;
Howard shall be Earl of Nottingham,
   And so was never Howard before.

"Now, Peter Simon, thou art old,
   I will maintain thee and thy son ;
Thou shalt have five hundred pound all in gold,
   For the good service that thou hast done."
Then King Henry shifted his room ;
   In came the queen and ladies bright,
Other errands had they none
   But to see Sir Andrew Barton, knight.

But when they see his deadly face,
   And his eyes were hollow in his head,
"I would give a hundred pound," says King Henry,
   " The man were alive as he is dead.
Yet for the manful part that he hath played,
   Both here and beyond the sea,
His men shall have half-a-crown a day
   To bring them to my brother, King Jamie."

Lord Thomas
and
Fair Annet

LORD Thomas and fair Annet
  Sate a' day on a hill ;
Whan night was come, and sun was set,
  They had not talked their fill.

Lord Thomas said a word in jest,
  Fair Annet took it ill :
" A' I will never wed a wife
  Against my ain friends will."

" Gif ye will never wed a wife,
  A wife will ne'er wed ye : "
Sae he is hame to tell his mither,
  And knelt upon his knee.

" O rede, O rede, mither," he says,
  " A gude rede gie to me :
O sall I tak the nut-brown bride,
  And let fair Annet be ? "

" The nut-brown bride haes gowd and gear,
  Fair Annet she has gat nane ;
And the little beauty fair Annet haes,
  O it wull soon be gane."

rede, advice.

And he has till his brother gane :
"Now, brother, rede ye me ;
A', sall I marry the nut-brown bride,
And let fair Annet be ? "

" The nut-brown bride has oxen, brother,
The nut-brown bride has kye :
I wad hae ye marry the nut-brown bride,
And cast fair Annet by."

" Her oxen may die i' the house, billie,
And her kye into the byre,
And I sall hae nothing to mysel',
But a fat fadge by the fire."

And he has till his sister gane :
"Now sister, rede ye me ;
O sall I marry the nut-brown bride,
And set fair Annet free ? "

" I'se rede ye tak fair Annet, Thomas,
And let the brown bride alane ;
Lest ye should sigh, and say, Alas,
What is this we brought hame ! "

" No, I will tak my mither's counsel,
And marry me out o' hand ;
And I will tak the nut-brown bride ;
Fair Annet may leave the land."

byre, cow-house.   fadge, hag.

Up then rose fair Annet's father,
  Twa hours or it were day,
And he is gane into the bower
  Wherein fair Annet lay.

" Rise up, rise up, fair Annet," he says,
  " Put on your silken sheen ;
Let us gae to St. Mary's kirk,
  And see that rich weddeen."

" My maids, gae to my dressing-room,
  And dress to me my hair ;
Where-e'er ye laid a plait before,
  See ye lay ten times mair.

" My maids, gae to my dressing-room,
  And dress to me my smock ;
The one half is o' the holland fine,
  The other o' needle-work."

The horse fair Annet rade upon,
  He amblit like the wind ;
Wi' siller he was shod before,
  Wi' burning gowd behind.

Four and twanty siller bells
  Were a' tied till his mane,
And yae tift o' the norland wind,
  They tinkled ane by ane.

sheen, shoes.   _tift_, puff.

Four and twanty gay gude knights
  Rade by fair Annet's side,
And four and twenty fair ladies,
  As gin she had bin a bride.

And whan she cam to Mary's kirk,
  She sat on Mary's stean :
The cleading that fair Annet had on
  It skinkled in their een.

And whan she cam into the kirk,
  She shimmer'd like the sun ;
The belt that was about her waist,
  Was a' wi' pearls bedone.

skinkled, sparkled.

She sat her by the nut-brown bride,
    And her een they were sae clear,
Lord Thomas he clean forgat the bride,
    When fair Annet drew near.

He had a rose into his hand,
    He gae it kisses three,
And reaching by the nut-brown bride,
    Laid it on fair Annet's knee.

Up than spak the nut-brown bride,
    She spak wi' mickle spite ;
" And where gat ye that rose-water,
    That does mak ye sae white ? "

" O I did get the rose-water
    Where ye wull ne'er get nane,
For I did get that very rose-water
    Into my mithers wame."

The bride she drew a long bodkin
    Frae out her gay head-gear,
And strake fair Annet unto the heart,
    That word spak never mair.

Lord Thomas he saw fair Annet wax pale,
    And marvelit what mote be :

wame, womb.

But whan he saw her dear heart's blude,
  A' wood-wroth wexed he.

He drew his dagger, that was sae sharp,
  That was sae sharp and meet,
And drave it into the nut-brown bride,
  That fell dead at his feet.

" Now stay for me, dear Annet," he said,
  " Now stay, my dear," he cried ;
Then strake the dagger until his heart,
  And fell dead by her side.

Lord Thomas was buried without kirk-wa',
  Fair Annet within the choir ;
And o' the tane there grew a birk,
  The other a bonny briar.

And ay they grew, and ay they threw,
  As they wad fain be near ;
And by this ye may ken right well,
  They were twa lovers dear.

          birk, birch.   *threw*, throve.

Leoffricus

LEOFFRICUS the noble earl,
  Of Chester, as I read,
Did for the city of Coventry
  Many a noble deed ;

Great privileges for the town
  This nobleman did get,
Of all things did make it so,
  That they toll free did sit,

Save only that for horses still
  They did some custom pay,
Which was great charges to the town
  Full long and many a day.

Wherefore his wife, Godiva fair,
  Did of the earl request,
That therefore he would make it free
  As well as all the rest.

And when the lady long had sued,
  Her purpose to obtain,
At last her noble Lord she took
  Within a pleasant vein,

And unto him with smiling cheer
  She did forthwith proceed,
Intreating greatly that he would
  Perform that godly deed.

" You move me much, fair dame," quoth he ;
    " Your suit I fain would shun ;
But what would you perform and do,
    To have the matter done ? "

" Why, anything, my lord," quoth she,
    " You will with reason crave,
I will perform it with goodwill
    If I my wish may have."

" If thou wilt grant one thing," he said,
    " Which I shall now require,
So soon as it is finished,
    Thou shalt have thy desire."

" Command what you think good, my lord ;
    I will thereto agree
On that condition, that this town
    In all things may be free."

" If thou wilt strip thy clothes off,
    And here wilt lay them down,
And at noonday on horseback ride,
    Stark naked through the town,

They shall be free for evermore.
    If thou wilt not do so,
More liberty than now they have
    I never will bestow."

The lady at this strange demand
  Was much abashed in mind ;
And yet for to fulfil this thing
  She ne'er a whit repined.

Wherefore to all the officers
  Of all the town she sent,
That they perceiving her good will
  Which for their weal was bent,

That on the day that she should ride,
  All persons through the town
Should keep their houses and shut their door,
  And clap their windows down,

So that no creature, young nor old,
  Should in the street be seen
Till she had ridden (all about)
  .Through all the city clean.

And when the day of riding came,
  No person did her see,
Saving her Lord, after which time
  The town was ever free.

William
≈ and ≈
Marjorie

LADY MARJORIE, Lady Marjorie,
  Sat sewing her silken seam,
And by her came a pale, pale ghost,
  Wi' mony a sigh and mane.

" Are ye my father, the king ? " she says,
  " Or are ye my brither John ?
Or are ye my true love, sweet William,
  From England newly come ? "

" I'm not your father, the king," he says,
  " No, no, nor your brither John ;
But I'm your true love, sweet William,
  From England that's newly come."

" Have ye brought me any scarlets sae red,
  Or any silks sae fine ;
Or have ye brought me any precious things,
  That merchants have for sale ? "

" I have not brought you any scarlets sae red,
  No, no, nor the silks sae fine ;
But I have brought you my winding-sheet
  O'er many's the rock and hill.

"O Lady Marjorie, Lady Marjorie,
  For faith and charitie,
Will ye give to me my faith and troth,
  That I gave once to thee?"

"O your faith and troth I'll not give thee,
  No, no, that will not I,
Until I get ae kiss of your ruby lips,
  And in my arms you come lie."

"My lips they are sae bitter," he says,
  "My breath it is sae strang,
If you get ae kiss of my ruby lips,
  Your days will not be lang.

"The cocks they are crawing, Marjorie," he
    says,—
  "The cocks they are crawing again;
It's time the dead should part the quick,—
  Marjorie, I must be gane."

She followed him high, she followed him low,
  Till she came to yon churchyard green;
O there the grave did open up,
  And young William he lay down.

"What three things are these, sweet William,"
    she says,
  "That stands here at your head?"
"It's three maidens, Marjorie," he says,
  "That I promised once to wed."

"What three things are these, sweet William,"
    she says,
  "That stands here at your side?"
"It is three babes, Marjorie," he says,
  "That these three maidens had."

"What three things are these, sweet William,"
    she says,
  "That stands here at your feet?"
"It is three hell-hounds, Marjorie," he says,
  "That's waiting my soul to keep."

She took up her white, white hand,
  And she struck him in the breast,
Saying,—"Have there again your faith and troth
  And I wish your soul gude rest."

The
≈ Gipsy Laddie

THE gipsies came to our good lord's gate,
  And wow but they sang sweetly;
They sang sae sweet and sae very complete,
  That down came the fair lady.

And she came tripping doun the stair,
  And a' her maids before her;
As soon as they saw her weel-far'd face,
  They coost the glamour o'er her.

" Gae tak frae me this gay mantle,
  And bring to me a plaidie ;
For if kith and kin and a' had sworn,
  I'll follow the gipsy laddie.

" Yestreen I lay in a weel-made bed,
  And my good lord beside me ;

E

This night I'll lie in a tennant's barn,
  Whatever shall betide me."

" Come to your bed," says Johnie Faa,
  " O come to your bed, my deary ;
For I vow and I swear by the hilt of my sword,
  That your lord shall nae mair come near ye."

" I'll go to bed to my Johnie Faa,
  I'll go to bed to my deary ;
For I vow and I swear, by what passed yestreen,
  That my lord shall nae mair come near me.

" I'll mak a hap to my Johnie Faa,
  And I'll mak a hap to my deary ;
And he's get a' the coat gaes round,
  And my lord shall nae mair come near me."

And when our lord came hame at e'en,
  And speir'd for his fair lady,
The tane she cried, and the other replied,
  " She's away wi' the gipsy laddie."

" Gae saddle to me the black black steed,
  Gae saddle and make him ready ;
Before that I either eat or sleep,
  I'll gae seek my fair lady."

And we were fifteen weel-made men,
  Altho' we were nae bonny ;
And we were a' put down for ane,
  A fair young wanton lady.

Waly,

Waly,

but

Love

be

Bonny

O WALY, waly up the bank,
   And waly, waly down the brae,
And waly, waly yon burn side,
   Where I and my love wont to gae.

I lean'd my back unto an aik,
   I thought it was a trusty tree ;
But first it bow'd, and syne it brak,
   Sae my true love did lightly me !

aik. oak.

O waly, waly, but love be bonny,
    A little time, while it is new ;
But when 'tis auld, it waxeth cauld,
    And fades away like morning dew.

O wherefore should I busk my head ?
    Or wherefore should I kame my hair ?
For my true love has me forsook,
    And says he'll never love me mair.

Now Arthur-Seat shall be my bed,
    The sheets shall ne'er be filed by me :
Saint Anton's well shall be my drink,
    Since my true love has forsaken me.

Martinmas wind, when wilt thou blaw,
    And shake the green leaves off the tree ?
O gentle death, when wilt thou come ?
    For of my life I am weary.

'Tis not the frost that freezes fell,
    Nor blawing snaw's inclemency ;
'Tis not sic cauld that makes me cry,
    But my love's heart grown cauld to me.

When we came in by Glasgow town,
    We were a comely sight to see ;
My love was clad in the black velvet,
    And I mysel' in cramasie.

filed, soiled.

But had I wist, before I kiss'd,
  That love had been sae ill to win,
I'd lock'd my heart in a case of gold,
  And pinn'd it with a silver pin.

Oh, oh, if my young babe were born,
  And set upon the nurse's knee,
And I mysel' were dead and gane!
  For a maid again I'll never be.

≋ The Bonny

Earl of Murray ≋

YE Highlands, and ye Lawlands,
  O where have you been?
They have slain the Earl of Murray,
  And they laid him on the green.

"Now wae be to thee, Huntly!
  And wherefore did you sae?
I bade you bring him wi' you,
  But forbade you him to slay."

He was a braw gallant,
  And he rid at the ring;
And the bonny Earl of Murray,
  O he might hae been a king.

He was a braw gallant,
   And he play'd at the ba' ;
And the bonny Earl of Murray
   Was the flower amang them a'.

He was a braw gallant,
   And he play'd at the glove ;
And the bonny Earl of Murray,
   O he was the Queen's love.

O lang will his lady
   Look o'er the castle Down,
Ere she see the Earl of Murray
   Come sounding thro' the town.

Glasgerion

GLASGERION was a king's own son,
   And a harper he was good ;
He harped in the king's chamber,
   Where cup and candle stood,

And so did he in the queen's chamber,
  Till ladies waxed wood,

And then bespake the king's daughter,
  And these words thus said she.

. . . . . .

Said " strike on, strike on, Glasgerion,
  Of thy striking do not blin ;
There's never a stroke comes over thine harp,
  But it glads my heart within."

" Fair might you fall, lady," quoth he,
  " Who taught you now to speak ?
I have loved you, lady, seven year ;
  My heart I durst ne'er break."

" But come to my bower, my Glasgerion,
  When all men are at rest ;
As I am a lady true of my promise,
  Thou shalt be a welcome guest."

But home then came Glasgerion,
  A glad man, Lord, was he :
And, " come thou hither, Jack, my boy,
  Come hither unto me.

" For the king's daughter of Normandy
  Her love is granted me ;
And before the cock have crowen
  At her chamber must I be."

blin, stop.

" But come you hither, master," quoth he,
" Lay your head down on this stone ;
For I will waken you, master dear,
Afore it be time to gone."

But up then rose that lither lad,
And did on hose and shoon ;
A collar he cast upon his neck,
He seemed a gentleman.

And when he came to that lady's chamber,
He tirled upon a pin :
The lady was true of her promise,
Rose up and let him in.

He did not take the lady gay,
To bolster nor to bed :
But down upon her chamber floor,
Full soon he hath her laid.

He did not kiss that lady gay
When he came nor when he youd :
And sore mistrusted that lady gay,
He was of some churlès blood.

But home then came that lither lad,
And did off his hose and shoon ;
And cast that collar from about his neck :
He was but a churlès son.
" Awaken," quoth he, " my master dear,
I hold it time to be gone.

lither, naughty.   youd, went (?).

" For I have saddled your horse, master,
    Well bridled I have your steed,
Have I not served a good breakfast,
    When time comes I have need."

But up then rose good Glasgerion,
    And did on hose and shoon,
And cast a collar about his neck :
    He was a kingés son.

And when he came to that lady's chamber,
    He tirled upon a pin ;
The lady was more than true of promise,
    Rose up and let him in.

Says " whether have you left with me
    Your bracelet or your glove ?
Or are you returned back again
    To know more of my love ? "

Glasgerion swore a full great oath,
    By oak, and ash, and thorn ;
" Lady, I was never in your chamber,
    Sith the time that I was born."

" O then it was your little foot-page,
    Falsely hath beguiled me : "
And then she pulled forth a little pen-knife,
    That hanged by her knee.
Says, " there shall never no churlès blood
    Spring within my body."

But home then went Glasgerion,
　A woe man, good [lord] was he.
Says, "come hither thou, Jack my boy,
　Come thou hither to me.

"For if I had killed a man to-night,
　Jack, I would tell it thee :
But if I have not killed a man to-night,
　Jack, thou hast killed three."

And he pulled out his bright brown sword,
　And dried it on his sleeve,
And he smote off that lither lad's head,
　And asked no man no leave.

He set the sword's point til his breast,
　The pummel till a stone :
Through that falseness of that lither lad,
　These three lives were all gone.

Fair
Margaret
and
Sweet
William.

As it fell out on a long summer's day,
   Two lovers they sat on a hill ;
They sat together that long summer's day,
   And could not talk their fill.

" I see no harm by you, Margaret,
   Nor you see none by me ;
Before to-morrow at eight o'clock
   A rich wedding you shall see."

Fair Margaret sat in her bower-window,
   Combing her yellow hair ;
There she spied sweet William and his bride,
   As they were a riding near.

Then down she laid her ivory comb,
   And braided her hair in twain :
She went alive out of her bower,
   But ne'er came alive in't again.

When day was gone, and night was come,
   And all men fast asleep,
Then came the spirit of fair Margaret,
   ` And stood at William's feet.

" Are you awake, sweet William ? " she said,
   " Or, sweet William, are you asleep ?
God give you joy of your gay bride-bed,
   And me of my winding-sheet."

When day was come, and night was gone,
   And all men wak'd from sleep,
Sweet William to his lady said,
   " My dear, I have cause to weep.

" I dreamt a dream, my dear lady,
   Such dreams are never good :
I dreamt my bower was full of red swine,
   And my bride-bed full of blood."

" Such dreams, such dreams, my honoured lord,
   They never do prove good ;
To dream thy bower was full of swine,
   And thy bride-bed full of blood."

He called up his merry men all,
   By one, by two, and by three ;
Saying, " I'll away to fair Margaret's bower,
   By the leave of my lady."

And when he came to fair Margaret's bower,
   He knocked at the ring ;
And who so ready as her seven brethren,
   To let sweet William in.

Then he turned up the covering-sheet ;
   " Pray let me see the dead ;
Methinks she does look pale and wan,
   She has lost her cherry red.

" I'll do more for thee, Margaret,
   Than any of thy kin :
For I will kiss thy pale wan lips,
   Though a smile I cannot win."

With that bespake the seven brethren,
  Making most piteous mone,
" You may go kiss your jolly brown bride,
  And let our sister alone."

" If I do kiss my jolly brown bride,
  I do but what is right ;
I ne'er made a vow to yonder poor corpse,
  By day, or yet by night.

" Deal on, deal on, my merry men all,
  Deal on your cake and your wine :
For whatever is dealt at her funeral to-day,
  Shall be dealt to-morrow at mine."

Fair Margaret died to-day, to-day,
  Sweet William died the morrow :
Fair Margaret died for pure true love,
  . Sweet William he died for sorrow.

Margaret was buried in the lower chancel,
  And William in the higher :
Out of her breast there sprang a rose,
  And out of his a briar.

They grew till they grew unto the church top,
  And then they could grow no higher ;
And then they tied in a true lover's knot,
  Which made all the people admire.

Then came the clerk of the parish,
As you this truth shall hear,
And by misfortune cut them down,
Or they had now been there.

--=|=|=---

≈ Edward,

≈ Edward

WHY does your brand sae drap wi' blood
Edward, Edward?
Why does your brand sae drap wi' blood
And why sae sad gang ye oh?
" Oh I hae killed my hawk sae good,
Mither, mither :
Oh I hae killed my hawk so good,
And I had no mair but he oh."

Your hawk's blood was never sae red,
Edward, Edward ;
Your hawk's blood was never sae red,
My dear son I tell thee oh.

" Oh I hae killed my red-roan steed,
                    Mither, mither :
Oh I hae killed my red roan steed
          That erst was sae fair and free oh."

Your steed was auld, and ye hae got mair,
                    Edward, Edward ;
Your steed was auld, and ye hae got mair,
          Some other dule ye dree oh.
" Oh I hae killed my father dear,
                    Mither, mither :
Oh I hae killed my father dear,
          Alas ! and wae is me oh ! "

And whatten penance will ye dree for that,
                    Edward, Edward ?
And whatten penance will ye dree for that ?
          My dear son, now tell me oh.
" I'll set my feet in yonder boat,
                    Mither, mither :
I'll set my feet in yonder boat,
          And I'll fare over the sea oh."

And what will ye do wi' your towers and
    your ha',
                    Edward, Edward ?
And what will ye do wi' your towers and
    your ha',
          That were sae fair to see oh ?

dule ye dree, woe ye die weeping.

"I'll let them stand till they down fa',
              Mither, mither :
I'll let them stand till they down fa',
       For here never mair maun I be oh."

And what will ye leave to your bairns and
    your wife,
              Edward, Edward?
And what will ye leave to your bairns and your
    wife,
       When ye gang over the sea oh?
"The world's room, let them beg through life,
              Mither, mither :
The world's room, let them beg through life,
       For them never mair will I see oh."

And what will ye leave to your ain mither dear,
              Edward, Edward?
And what will ye leave to your ain mither dear,
              My dear son, now tell me oh.
"The curse of hell frae me shall ye bear,
              Mither, mither :
The curse of hell frae me shall ye bear,
       Sic counsels ye gave to me oh."

Young ≋
Waters ≋

ABOUT Yule, when the wind blew cool ;
　And the round tables began,
A' there is come to our king's court
　Mony a well-favoured man.

The queen looked o'er the castle wa',
　Beheld baith dale and down,
And then she saw young Waters
　Come riding to the town.

His footmen they did rin before,
　His horsemen rade behind ;
Ane mantle of the burning gowd
　Did keep him frae the wind.

Gowden graith'd his horse before,
　And siller shod behind ;
The horse young Waters rade upon
　Was fleeter than the wind.

Out then spake a wily lord,
　Unto the queen said he :
" O tell me wha's the fairest face
　Rides in the company ? "

graith'd, girthed.

"I've seen lord, and I've seen laird,
   And knights of high degree,
But a fairer face than young Waters
   Mine eyen did never see."

Out then spake the jealous king
   And an angry man was he :
"O if he had been twice as fair,
   You might have excepted me." ·

"You're neither laird nor lord," she says,
   "But the king that wears the crown ;
There is not a knight in fair Scotland,
   But to thee maun bow down."

For a' that she could do or say,
   Appeased he wad nae be ;
But for the words which she had said,
   Young Waters he maun dee.

They hae ta'en young Waters,
   And put fetters to his feet ;
They hae ta'en young Waters,
   And thrown him in dungeon deep.

"Aft I have ridden thro' Stirling town,
   In the wind but and the weet ;
But I ne'er rade thro' Stirling town
   Wi' fetters at my feet.

" Aft have I ridden thro' Stirling town,
   In the wind but and the rain ;
But I ne'er rade thro' Stirling town
   Ne'er to return again."

They hae ta'en to the heading-hill
   His young son in his cradle ;
And they hae ta'en to the heading-hill
   His horse but and his saddle.

They hae ta'en to the heading-hill
   His lady fair to see ;
And for the words the queen had spoke
   Young Waters he did dee.

Children in the Wood

Now ponder well, you parents dear,
   These words which I shall write ;
A doleful story you shall hear,
   In time brought forth to light.

heading, beheading.

A gentleman of good account
  In Norfolk dwelt of late,
Who did in honour far surmount
  Most men of his estate.

Sore sick he was, and like to die,
  No help his life could save ;
His wife by him as sick did lie,
  And both possessed one grave.
No love between these two was lost,
  Each was to other kind ;
In love they liv'd, in love they died,
  And left two babes behind :

The one a fine and pretty boy,
  Not passing three years old ;
The other a girl more young than he,
  And fram'd in beauty's mould.
The father left his little son,
  As plainly doth appear,
When he to perfect age should come,
  Three hundred pounds a year.

And to his little daughter Jane
  Five hundred pounds in gold,
To be paid down on marriage-day,
  Which might not be controll'd :
But if the children chance to die,
  Ere they to age should come,
Their uncle should possess their wealth ;
  For so the will did run.

" Now, brother," said the dying man,
   " Look to my children dear ;
Be good unto my boy and girl,
   No friends else have they here :
To God and you I recommend
   My children dear this day ;
But little while be sure we have
   Within this world to stay.

" You must be father and mother both,
   And uncle all in one ;
God knows what will become of them,
   When I am dead and gone."
With that bespake their mother dear,
   " O brother kind," quoth she,
" You are the man must bring our babes
   To wealth or misery :

" And if you keep them carefully,
   Then God will you reward ;
But if you otherwise should deal,
   God will your deeds regard."
With lips as cold as any stone,
   They kissed their children small :
" God bless you both, my children dear ; "
   With that the tears did fall.

These speeches then their brother spake
   To this sick couple there :
" The keeping of your little ones,
   Sweet sister, do not fear.

God never prosper me nor mine,
  Nor aught else that I have,
If I do wrong your children dear,
  When you are laid in grave."

The parents being dead and gone,
  The children home he takes,
And brings them straight unto his house,
  Where much of them he makes.
He had not kept these pretty babes
  A twelvemonth and a day,
But, for their wealth, he did devise
  To make them both away.

He bargain'd with two ruffians strong,
  Which were of furious mood,
That they should take these children young,
  And slay them in a wood.
He told his wife an artful tale.
  He would the children send
To be brought up in fair London,
  With one that was his friend.

Away then went those pretty babes,
  Rejoicing at that tide,
Rejoicing with a merry mind,
  They should on cock-horse ride.
They prate and prattle pleasantly,
  As they rode on the way,
To those that should their butchers be,
  And work their lives decay :

So that the pretty speech they had,
  Made Murder's heart relent :
And they that undertook the deed,
  Full sore did now repent.
Yet one of them more hard of heart,
  Did vow to do his charge,
Because the wretch, that hired him,
  Had paid him very large.

The other won't agree thereto,
  So here they fall to strife ;
With one another they did fight,
  About the children's life :
And he that was of mildest mood,
  Did slay the other there,
Within an unfrequented wood ;
  The babes did quake for fear !

He took the children by the hand,
  Tears standing in their eye,
And bad them straightway follow him,
  And look they did not cry :
And two long miles he led them on,
  While they for food complain :
"Stay here," quoth he, "I'll bring you bread,
  When I come back again."

These pretty babes, with hand in hand,
  Went wandering up and down ;
But never more could see the man
  Approaching from the town :

Their pretty lips with blackberries,
  Were all besmear'd and dyed,
And when they saw the darksome night,
  They sat them down and cried.

Thus wandered these poor innocents,
  Till death did end their grief,
In one another's arms they died,
  As wanting due relief :
No burial this pretty pair
  Of any man receives,
Till Robin-red-breast piously
  Did cover them with leaves.

And now the heavy wrath of God,
  Upon their uncle fell ;
Yea, fearful fiends did haunt his house,
  His conscience felt an hell ;
His barns were fir'd, his goods consum'd,
  His lands were barren made,
His cattle died within the field,
  And nothing with him stayed.

And in the voyage of Portugal [1]
  Two of his sons did die ;
And to conclude, himself was brought
  To want and misery :
He pawn'd and mortgaged all his land
  Ere seven years came about,
And now at length this wicked act
  Did by this means come out :

[1] Percy has 'to' but Ritson points out that it should be 'of.'

The fellow, that did take in hand
　These children for to kill,
Was for a robbery judg'd to die,
　Such was God's blessed will :
Who did confess the very truth,
　As here hath been display'd :
Their uncle having died in gaol,
　Where he for debt was laid.

You that executors be made,
　And overseers eke
Of children that be fatherless,
　And infants mild and meek ;
Take you example by this thing,
　And yield to each his right,
Lest God with such like misery
　Your wicked minds requite.

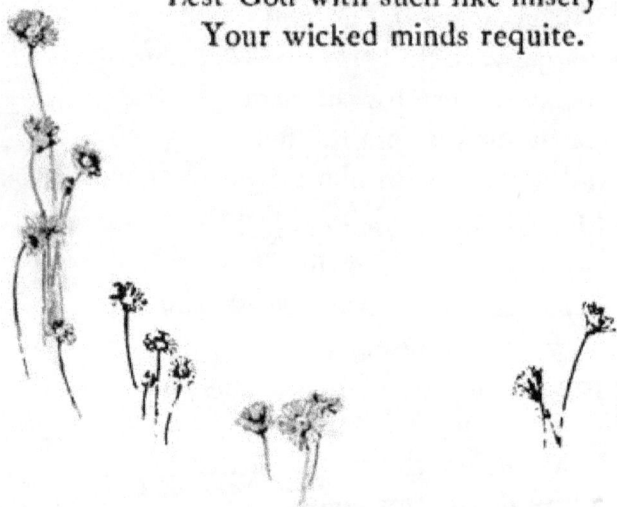

≈ Hugh
of Lincoln ≈

Four and twenty bonny boys
  Were playing at the ba';
And by it came him, sweet Sir Hugh,
  And he play'd o'er them a'.

He kick'd the ba' with his right foot,
  And catch'd it wi' his knee;
And through-and-through the Jew's window,
  He gar'd the bonny ba' flee.

He's done him to the Jew's castle,
  And walk'd it round about;
And there he saw the Jew's daughter
  At the window looking out.

" Throw down the ba', ye Jew's daughter,
  Throw down the ba' to me!"
" Never a bit," says the Jew's daughter,
  " Till up to me come ye."

" How will I come up? How can I come up?
  How can I come to thee?
For as ye did to my auld father,
  The same ye'll do to me."

gar'd, made.

She's gane till her father's garden,
    And pu'd an apple, red and green ;
'Twas a' to wile him, sweet Sir Hugh,
    And to entice him in.

She's led him in through ae dark door,
    And sae has she through nine ;
She's laid him on a dressing table,
    And stickit him like a swine.

And first came out the thick, thick blood,
    And syne came out the thin ;
And syne came out the bonny heart's blood ;
    There was nae mair within.

She's row'd him in a cake o' lead,
    Bade him lie still and sleep ;
She's thrown him in Our Lady's draw well,
    Was fifty fathom deep.

When bells were rung, and mass was sung,
    And a' the bairns came hame,
When every lady gat hame her son,
    The Lady Maisry gat nane.

She's ta'en her mantle her about,
    Her coffer by the hand ;
And she's gane out to seek her son,
    And wander'd o'er the land.

row'd, rolled.

She's done her to the Jew's castle,
  Where a' were fast asleep ;
" Gin ye be there, my sweet Sir Hugh,
  I pray you to me speak."

She's done her to the Jew's garden,
  Thought he had been gathering fruit ;
" Gin ye be there, my sweet Sir Hugh,
  I pray you to me speak."

She near'd Our Lady's deep draw-well,
  Was fifty fathom deep ;
" Where'er ye be, my sweet Sir Hugh,
  I pray you to me speak."

" Gae hame, gae hame, my mither dear ;
  Prepare my winding sheet ;
And, at the back o' merry Lincoln,
  The morn I will you meet."

Now Lady Maisry is gane hame ;
  Made him a winding sheet ;
And, at the back o' merry Lincoln,
  The dead corpse did her meet.

And a' the bells o' merry Lincoln,
  Without men's hands were rung ;
And a' the books o' merry Lincoln,
  Were read without man's tongue ;
And ne'er was such a burial
  Sin Adam's days begun.

Sir
Patrick
Spence
ξ

THE king sits in Dumferling toun,
  Drinking the blude-red wine :
" O where will I get guid sailor,
  To sail this ship of mine ? "

Up and spak an eldern knight,
  Sat at the king's right knee :
" Sir Patrick Spence is the best sailor,
  That sails upon the sea."

The king has written a braid letter,
  And signed it wi' his hand,
And sent it to Sir Patrick Spence,
  Was walking on the sand.

The first line that Sir Patrick read,
  A loud laugh laughed he :
The next line that Sir Patrick read,
  The tear blinded his ee.

" O wha is this has done this deed,
  This ill deed done to me ;
To send me out this time o' the year,
  To sail upon the sea ?

" Mak haste, mak haste, my merry men all,
  Our guid ship sails the morn."
" O say na sae, my master dear,
  For I fear a deadly storm.

" Late late yestreen I saw the new moon
  Wi' the auld moon in her arm ;
And I fear, I fear, my dear master,
  That we will come to harm."

O our Scots nobles were right loath
  To wet their cork-heeled shoon ;
But lang ere a' the play were playd,
  Their hats they swam aboon.

O lang, lang, may their ladies sit
  Wi' their fans into their hand,
Or e'er they see Sir Patrick Spence
  Come sailing to the land.

O lang, lang, may the ladies stand
  Wi' their gold kems in their hair,
Waiting for their ain dear lords,
  For they'll see them na mair.

shoon, shoes,

Half o'er, half o'er to Aberdour,
  It's fifty fathom deep :
And there lies guid Sir Patrick Spence,
  Wi' the Scots lords at his feet.

Child

Waters

CHILD Waters in his stable stood
  And stroked his milk-white steed ;
To him came a fair yong lady
  As ever did wear womans weed.

Says, "Christ you save, good Child Waters,"
  Says, "Christ you save and see ;
My girdle of gold which was too long,
  Is now too short for me.

"And all is with one child of yours
  I feel stir at my side ;

weed, dress.

My gown of green it is too straight ;
  Before, it was too wide."

" If the child be mine, fair Ellen," he said,
  " Be mine, as you tell me,
Take you Cheshire and Lancashire both,
  Take them your own to be.

" If the child be mine, fair Ellen," he said,
  " Be mine, as you do swear,
Take you Cheshire and Lancashire both,
  And make that child your heir."

She says, " I had rather have one kiss,
  Child Waters, of thy mouth,
Than I would have Cheshire and Lancashire both,
  That lies by north and south.

" And I had rather have a twinkling,
  Child Waters, of your ee,
Than I would have Cheshire and Lancashire both,
  To take them mine own to be."

" To morrow, Ellen, I must forth ride
  Far into the north countree ;
The fairest lady that I can find,
  Ellen, must go with me."
" And ever I pray you, Child Waters,
  Your foot-page let me be."

G

"If you will my foot-page be, Ellen,
　As you do tell it me,
Then you must cut your gown of green
　An inch above your knee :

"So must you do your yellow locks,
　Another inch above your ee ;
You must tell no man what is my name ;
　My foot-page then you shall be."

All this long day Child Waters rode,
　She ran barefoot by his side,
Yet he was never so courteous a knight,
　To say, "Ellen, will you ride ?"

But all this day Child Waters rode,
　She ran barefoot through the broom,
Yet he was never so courteous a knight,
　As to say, "put on your shoon."

"Ride softly," she said, "Child Waters
　Why do you ride so fast ?
The child, which is no man's but yours,
　My body it will burst."

He says, "sees thou yonder water, Ellen,
　That flows from bank to brim ?"
"I trust to God, Child Waters," she said,
　"You will never see me swim.

But when she came to the water's side,
  She sailed to the chin :
" Except the Lord of heaven be my speed,
  Now must I learn to swim."

The salt waters bare up Ellen's clothes,
  Our Lady bare up her chin ;
Child Waters was a woe man, good Lord,
  To see fair Ellen swim !

And when she over the water was,
  She then came to his knee :
He said, " Come hither, fair Ellen,
  Lo yonder what I see.

" Seest thou not yonder hall, Ellen ?
  Of red gold shine the gates :
There's four and twenty fair ladies,
  The fairest is my worldly make.

" Seest thou not yonder hall, Ellen ?
  Of red gold shineth the tower :
There is four and twenty fair ladies,
  The fairest is my paramour."

" I do see the hall now, Child Waters,
  That of red gold shineth the gates :
God give good then of yourself,
  And of your worldly make.

male, mate.

"I do see the hall now, Child Waters,
    That of red gold shineth the tower :
God give good then of yourself,
    And of your paramour."

There were four and twenty ladies
    Were playing at the ball,
And Ellen, was the fairest lady,
    Must bring his steed to the stall.

There were four and twenty fair ladies
    Was a playing at the chess,
And Ellen, she was the fairest lady,
    Must bring his horse to grass.

And then bespake Child Water's sister,
    And these were the words said she :
"You have the prettiest foot-page, brother,
    That ever I saw with mine eye.

"But that his belly it is so big,
    His girdle goes wondrous high ;
And ever, I pray you, Child Waters,
    Let him go into the chamber with me."

"It is more meet for a little foot-page,
    That has run through moss and mire,
To take his supper upon his knee,
    And sit down by the kitchen fire,
Then to go into the chamber with any lady,
    That wears so [rich] attire."

But when they had supped every one,
　To bed they took the way :
He said, " Come hither, my little foot-page,
　Hearken what I do say.

" And go thee down into yonder town,
　And low into the street ;
The fairest lady that thou canst find,
　Hire her in mine arms to sleep ;
And take her up in thine arms two,
　For filing of her feet."

Ellen is gone into the town,
　And low into the street ;
The fairest lady that she could find,
　She hired in his arms to sleep ;
And took her up in her arms two,
　For filing of her feet.

" I pray you now, good Child Waters,
　That I may creep in at your bed's feet ;
For there is no place about this house,
　Where I may say a sleep."

This [night] and it drove on afterward,
　Till it was near the day,
He said, " Rise up, my little foot-page,
　And give my steed corn and hay ;
And so do thou the good black oats,
　That he may carry me the better away."

And up then rose fair Ellen,
   And gave his steed corn and hay ;
And so she did and the good black oats,
   That he might carry him the better away.

She leaned her back to the manger side,
   And grievously did groan ;
And that beheard his mother dear,
   And heard her make her moan.

She said, " Rise up, thou Child Waters,
   I think thou art a cursed man ;
For yonder is a ghost in thy stable,
   That grievously doth groan ;
Or else some woman labours of child,
   She is so woe-begone."

But up then rose Child Waters,
   And did on his shirt of silk ;
Then he put on his other clothes,
   On his body as white as milk.

And when he came to the stable door,
   Full still that he did stand,
That he might hear now fair Ellen,
   How she made her monand.

She said, " Lullaby, my own dear child,
   Lullaby, dear child, dear ;
I would thy father were a king,
   Thy mother laid on a bier."

monand, moaning.

"Peace now," he said, "good, fair Ellen,
 And be of good cheer, I thee pray ;
And the bridal and the churching both
 They shall be upon one day."

Earl

Richard

EARL RICHARD once upon a day,
 And all his valiant men so wight,
He did him down to Barnisdale,·
 Where all the land is fair and light.

He was aware of a damosel,
 I wot fast on she did her bound,
With towers of gold upon her head,
 As fair a woman as could be found.

He said, "Busk on you, fair lady,
 The white flowers and the red ;
For I would give my bonnie ship,
 To get your maidenhead."

"I wish your bonnie ship rent and rive,
 And drown you in the sea ;
For all this would not mend the miss
 That ye would do to me."
"The miss is not so great, lady,
 Soon mended it might be.

"I have four-and-twenty mills in Scotland,
 Stands on the water of Tay ;
You'll have them, and as much flour
 As they'll grind in a day."

"I wish your bonnie ship rent and rive,
 And drown you in the sea ;
For all that would not mend the miss
 That ye would do to me."
"The miss is not so great, lady,
 Soon mended it will be.

"I have four-and-twenty milk-white cows,
 All calved in a day ;
You'll have them, and as much hained grass
 As they all on can gae."

"I wish your bonnie ship rent and rive,
 And drown you in the sea ;
For all that would not mend the miss
 That ye would do to me."
"The miss is not so great, lady,
 Soon mended it might be.

hained, enclosed.

"I have four-and-twenty milk-white steeds,
    All foaled in one year ;
You'll have them, and as much red gold
    As all their backs can bear."

She turned her right and round about,
    And she swore by the mould,
"I would not be your love," said she,
    "For that church full of gold."

He turned him right and round about,
    And he swore by the mass,
Says,—"Lady, ye my love shall be,
    And gold ye shall have less."

She turned her right and round about,
    And she swore by the moon,
"I would not be your love," says she,
    "For all the gold in Rome."

He turned him right and round about,
    And he swore by the moon,
Says,—"Lady, ye my love shall be,
    And gold ye shall have none."

He caught her by the milk-white hand,
    And by the grass-green sleeve ;
And there has taken his will of her,
    Wholly without her leave.

The lady frowned and sadly blushed,
　　And oh ! but she thought shame :
Says,—" If you are a knight at all,
　　You surely will tell me your name."

" In some places they call me Jack,
　　In other some they call me John ;
But when into the Queen's Court,
　　Oh then Lithcock it is my name."

" Lithcock ! Lithcock ! " the lady said,
　　And oft she spelt it over again ;
" Lithcock ! it's Latin," the lady said,
　　" Richard's the English of that name."

The knight he rode, the lady ran,
　　A live long summer's day ;
Till they came to the wan water
　　That all men do call Tay.

He set his horse head to the water,
　　Just thro' it for to ride ;
And the lady was as ready as him
　　The waters for to wade.

For he had never been as kind-hearted
　　As to bid the lady ride ;
And she had never been so low-hearted
　　As for to bid him bide.

But deep into the wan water
  There stands a great big stone ;
He turned his wight horse head about,
  Said, " Lady fair, will ye loup on ? "

She's taken the wand was in her hand,
  And struck it on the foam,
And before he got the middle stream,
  The lady was on dry land.
" By help of God and our Lady,
  My help lies not in your hand.

" I learned it from my mother dear,—
  Few are there that have learned better—
When I come to deep water,
  I can swim thro' like any otter.

" I learned it from my mother dear,—
  I find I learned it for my weel ;
When I come to a deep water,
  I can swim thro' like any eel."

" Turn back, turn back, you lady fair,
  You know not what I see ;
There is a lady in that castle,
  That will burn you and me."
" Betide me weal, betide me wae,
  That lady I will see."

  wight, active.

She took a ring from her finger,
   And gave't the porter for his fee :
Says, " Take you that, my good porter,
   And bid the Queen speak to me."

And when she came before the Queen,
   There she fell low down on her knee :
Says, " There is a knight into your court,
   This day has robbed me."

" O has he robbed you of your gold,
   Or has he robbed you of your fee ? "
" He has not robbed me of my gold,
   He has not robbed me of my fee ;
He has robbed me of my maidenhead,
   The fairest flower of my body."

" There is no knight in all my court,
   That thus has robbed thee,
But you'll have the truth of his right hand,
   Or else for your sake he'll die,
Tho' it were Earl Richard, my own brother ;
   And oh forbid that it be ! "
Then, sighing, said the lady fair,
   " I wot the same man is he."

The Queen called on her merry men,
   Even fifty men and three ;
Earl Richard used to be the first man,
   But now the hindmost man was he.

He's taken out one hundred pounds,
  And told it in his glove :
Says, " Take you that, my lady fair,
  And seek another love."

" Oh no, oh no," the lady cried,
  " That's what shall never be ;
I'll have the truth of your right hand,
  The Queen it gave to me."

" I wish I had drunk of your water, sister,
  When I did drink your wine ;
That for a carl's fair daughter,
  It does gar me dree all this pine."

" May be I am a carl's daughter,
  And may be never nane ;
When ye met me in the green wood,
  Why did you not let me alane ? "

" Will you wear the short clothes,
  Or will you wear the side ;
Or will you walk to your wedding,
  Or will you till it ride ? "

" I will not wear the short clothes,
  But I will wear the side ;
I will not walk to my wedding,
  But I to it will ride."

carl, churl. _gar_, make. _dree_, mourn. _pine_, woe. _side_, long.

When he was set upon the horse,
    The lady him behin',
Then cauld and eerie were the words
    The twa had them between.

She said, " Good e'en, ye nettles tall,
    Just there where ye grow at the dike ;
If the auld carline my mother was here,
    Sae weel's she would your pates pike.

" How she would stap you in her poke,
    I wot at that she wadna fail ;
And boil ye in her auld brass pan,
    And of ye make right good kail.

" And she would meal you with millering
    That she gathers at the mill,
And make you thick as any dough ;
    And when the pan was brimful,

" Would mess you up in scuttle dishes,
    Syne bid us sup till we were fou ;
Lay down her head upon a poke.
    Then sleep and snore like any sow."

" Away ! away ! you bad woman,
    For all your vile words grieveth me ;
When ye hide so little for yourself,
    I'm sure ye'll hide far less for me.

pile, pick.   *stap*, stuff.   *poke*, bag.   *kail*, broth.
scuttle-dish, wooden platter.

"I wish I had drunk your water, sister,
    When that I did drink of your wine ;
Since for a carl's fair daughter,
    It aye gars me dree all this pine."

"May be I am a carl's daughter,
    And may be never nane ;
When ye met me in the good green wood,
    Why did you not let me alane ?

"Gude e'en, gude e'en, ye heather berries,
    As ye're growing on yon hill ;
If the auld carline and her bags were here,
    I wot she would get meat her fill.

"Late, late at night I knit our pokes,
    With even four-and-twenty knots ;
And in the morn at breakfast time,
    I'll carry the keys of an earl's locks.

"Late, late at night I knit our pokes,
    With even four-and-twenty strings ;
And if you look to my white fingers,
    They have as many gay gold rings."

"Away ! away ! ye ill woman,
    So sore your vile words grieveth me ;
When you hide so little for yourself,
    I'm sure ye'll hide far less for me.

" But if you are a carl's daughter,
    As I take you to be,
How did you get the gay clothing,
    In green wood ye had on thee ? "

" My mother she's a poor woman,
    She nursed earl's children three ;
And I got them from a foster sister,
    For to beguile such sparks as thee."

" But if you be a carl's daughter,
    As I believe you be,
How did you learn the good Latin,
    In green wood ye spoke to me ? "

" My mother she's a mean woman,
    She nursed earl's children three ;
I learned it from their chaplain,
    To beguile such sparks as ye."

When mass was sung, and bells were rung,
    And all men bound for bed,
Then Earl Richard and this lady
    In ae bed they were laid.

He turned his face unto the stock,
    And she hers to the stane ;
And cauld and dreary was the love
    That was these twa between.

Great mirth was in the kitchen,
　　Likewise intill the ha' ;
But in his bed lay Earl Richard,
　　Wiping the tears awa'.

He wept till he fell fast asleep,
　　Then slept till light was come ;
Then he did hear the gentlemen
　　That talked in the room :

Said,—"Saw ye ever a fitter match,
　　Betwixt the ane and ither ;
The King o' Scotland's fair dochter,
　　And the Queen of England's brither ? "

" And is she the King o' Scotland's fair
　　dochter ?
　　This day, oh, weel is me !
For seven times has my steed been saddled,
　　To come to court with thee ;
And with this witty lady fair,
　　How happy must I be ! "

Adam

Bel,

Clym

of the

Clough,

and

William

of

Cloudesle

č

MERRY it was in green forest,
  Among the leaves green,
Where that men walk east and west,
  With bows and arrows keen.

To raise the deer out of their den,—
  Such sights hath oft been seen,—
As by three yeomen of the north country,
  By them it is I mean.

The one of them hight Adam Bel,
　　The other Clym of the Clough,
The third was William of Cloudesle,
　　An archer good enough.

They were outlawed for venison,
　　These yeomen every one ;
They swore them brethren upon a day,
　　To English-wood for to gone.

Now lith and listen, gentlemen,
　　That of mirths loveth to hear :
Two of them were single men,
　　The third had a wedded fere.

William was the wedded man,
　　Much more then was his care :
He said to his brethren upon a day,
　　To Carlisle he would fare,

For to speak with fair Alice his wife,
　　And with his children three.
" By my troth," said Adam Bel,
　　" Not by the counsel of me.

" For if ye go to Carlisle, brother,
　　And from this wild wood wend,
If the justice may you take,
　　Your life were at an end."

hight, was called.　　　*lith*, listen.　　　*fere*, mate.

" If that I come not tomorrow, brother,
    By prime to you again,
Trust not else but that I am take,
    Or else that I am slain."

He took his leave of his brethren two,
    And to Carlisle he is gone ;
There he knocked at his own window,
    Shortly and anon.

" Where be you, fair Alice, my wife,
    And my children three ?
Lightly let in thine own husband,
    William of Cloudeslè."

" Alas ! " then said fair Alice,
    And sighed wondrous sore,
" This place hath been beset for you,
    This half year and more."

" Now am I here," said Cloudeslè,
    " I would that I in were :—
Now fetch us meat and drink enough,
    And let us make good cheer."

She fetched him meat and drink plenty,
    Like a true wedded wife,
And pleased him with that she had,
    Whom she loved as her life.

There lay an old wife in that place,
  A little beside the fire,
Which William had found, of charity,
  More than seven year.

Up she rose and walked full still,
  Evil mote she sped therefore,
For she had not set no foot on ground
  In seven year before.

She went unto the justice hall,
  As fast as she could hie ;
" This night is come unto this town
  William of Cloudeslè."

Thereof the iustice was full fain,
  And so was the sheriff also ;
" Thou shalt not travel hither, dame, for nought,
  Thy meed thou shalt have or thou go."

They gave to her a right good gown,
  Of scarlet it was, as I heard sayen ;
She took the gift and home she went,
  And couched her down again.

They raised the town of merry Carlisle,
  In all the haste that they can,
And came thronging to William's house,
  As fast as they might gone.

found—i.e. found for, provided for.   *still*, quietly

There they beset that good yeoman,
  Round about on every side,
William heard great noise of folks,
  That hitherward they hied.

Alice opened a shot-window,
  And looked all about,
She was ware of the justice and sheriff both,
  With a full great rout.

"Alas! treason," cried Alice.
  "Ever woe may thou be!
Go into my chamber, my husband," she said,
  "Sweet William of Cloudeslè."

He took his sword and his buckler,
  His bow and his children three,
And went into his strongest chamber,
  Where he thought surest to be.

Fair Alice followed him as a lover true,
  With a pollaxe in her hand;
"He shall be dead that here cometh in
  This door, while I may stand."

Cloudeslè bent a well good bow,
  That was of trusty tree,
He smote the justice on the breast,
  That his arrow burst in three.

shot-window, projecting window.

" God's curse on his heart," said William,
  " This day thy coat did on ;
If it had been no better than mine,
  It had gone near thy bone."

" Yield thee, Cloudeslè," said the justice,
  " And thy bow and thy arrows thee fro : "
" God's curse on his heart," said fair Alice,
  " That my husband counselleth so."

" Set fire on the house," said the sheriff,
  " Sith it will no better be,
And we burn therein William," he said,
  " His wife and children three."

They fired the house in many a place,
  The fire flew up on high ;
" Alas ! " then cried fair Alice,
  " I see we here shall die."

William opened his back window,
  That was in his chamber on high,
And with sheets let his wife down,
  And his children three.

" Have here my treasure," said William,
  " My wife and my children three,
For Christ's love do them no harm,
  But wreak you all on me."

William shot so wondrous well,
  Till his arrows were all ygo,
And the fire so fast upon him fell,
  That his bowstring brent in two.

The spercles brent and fell him on,
  Good William of Cloudeslè !
But then wax he a woeful man,
  And said, " this is a coward's death to me.

" Liever I had," said William,
  " With my sword in the rout to renne,
Then here among mine ennemies wode,
  Thus cruelly to bren."

He took his sword and his buckler,
  And among them all he ran ;
Where the people were most in press,
  He smote down many a man.

There might no man stand his stroke,
  So fiercely on them he ran ;
Then they threw windows and doors on him,
  And so took that good yeomàn.

There they him bound both hand and foot,
  And in deep dungeon him cast ;
" Now, Cloudeslè," said the high justice,
  " Thou shalt be hanged in haste."

ygo, gone.   *brent,* burst and burnt.   *spercles,* sparks.   *renne,* run.
            wode, fierce.   *press,* crowd.

" One vow shall I make," said the sheriff,
    " A pair of new gallows shall I for thee make,
And the gates of Carlisle shall be shut,
    There shall no man come in thereat.

" Then shall not help Clym of the Clough,
    Nor yet shall Adam Bel,
Though they came with a thousand more,
    Nor all the devils in hell."

Early in the morning the justice uprose,
    To the gates first gan he gone,
And commanded to be shut full close
    Lightilè everyone.

Then went he to the market place,
    As fast as he could hie ;
A pair of new gallows there did he up set,
    Beside the pillory.

A little boy stood them among,
    And asked what meaned that gallow tree ;
They said, " to hang a good yeomàn,
    Called William of Cloudeslè."

That little boy was the town swine-herd,
    And kept fair Alice swine,
Oft he had seen Cloudeslè in the wood,
    And given him there to dine.

lightilè, quickly.

He went out at a crevice in the wall,
  And lightly to the wood did gone ;
There met he with these wight young men,
  Shortly and anon.

" Alas ! " then said that little boy,
  " Ye tarry here all too long ;
Cloudeslè is taken and damned to death,
  All ready for to hong."

" Alas ! " then said good Adam Bel,
  " That ever we see this day !
He might here with us have dwelled,
  So oft as we did him pray !

" He might have tarried in green forest,
  Under the shadows sheen,
And have kept both him and us in rest,
  Out of trouble and teen ! "

Adam bent a right good bow,
  A great hart soon had he slain ;
" Take that, child," he said, " to thy dinner,
  And bring me mine arrow again."

" Now go we hence," said these wight young
      men,
  " Tarry we no longer here ;
We shall him borrow, by God's grace,
  Though we buy it full dear."

teen, woe.   *borrow*, rescue.

To Carlisle went these good yeomèn,
   On a merry morning of May :
Here is a fit of Cloudeslè,
   And another is for to say.

[THE SECOND FIT.]

AND when they came to merry Carlisle,
   In a fair morning tide,
They found the gates shut them until,
   Round about on every side.

" Alas ! " then said good Adam Bell,
   " That ever we were made men !
These gates be shut so wonderly well,
   That we may not come here in."

Then spake him Clym of the Clough,
   " With a wile we will us in bring ;
Let us say we be messengers,
   Straight comen from our king."

Adam said, " I have a letter written well,
   Now let us wisely work ;
We will say we have the king's seal,
   I hold the porter no clerk."

Then Adam Bel beat on the gate,
   With strokes great and strong ;
The porter heard such noise thereat,
   And to the gate fast he throng.

                throng, hurried.

" Who is there now," said the porter,
    " That maketh all this knocking ?
" We be two messengers," said Clym of the
        Clough,
    " Be comen straight from our king."

" We have a letter," said Adam Bel,
    " To the justice we must it bring ;
Let us in, our message to do,
    That we were again to our king."

" Here cometh no man in," said the porter,
    " By Him that died on a tree,
Till a false thief be hanged,
    Called William of Cloudeslè."

Then spake the good yeoman Clym of the Clough,
    And swore by Mary free,
" And if that we stand long without,
    Like a thief hanged shalt thou be.

" Lo here we have the king's seal ;
    What ! lordeyne, art thou wode ? "
The porter wend it had been so,
    And lightly did off his hode.

" Welcome be my lord's seal," he said,
    " For that ye shall come in :"
He opened the gate full shortly,
    An evil opening for him.

> *free*, gracious.   *lordeyne*, clown.   *wode*, mad.
>   *wend*, weened, thought.   *hode*, hood.

" Now are we in," said Adam Bel,
   " Thereof we are full fain,
But Christ knoweth that harrowed hell,
   How we shall come out again."

" Had we the keys," said Clym of the Clough,
   " Right well then should we speed ;
Then might we come out well enough,
   When we see time and need."

They called the porter to a council,
   And wrang his neck in two,
And cast him in a deep dungeon,
   And took his keys him fro.

" Now am I porter," said Adam Bel,
   " See, brother, the keys have we here ;
The worst porter to merry Carlisle,
   That ye had this hundred year.

" And now will we our bows bend,
   Into the town will we go,
For to deliver our dear brother,
   That liveth in care and woe."

[And thereupon] they bent their bows,
   And looked their strings were round ;
The market place of merry Carlisle,
   They beset in that stound.

                    stound, hour.

And as they looked them beside,
  A pair of new gallows there they see,
And the justice with a quest of swearers,
  That had judged Cloudeslè there hanged to be.

And Cloudeslé himself lay ready in a cart,
  Fast bound both foot and hand,
And a strong rope about his neck,
  All ready for to be hanged.

The justice called to him a lad,
  Cloudeslès clothes should he have,
To take the measure of that good yeoman,
  And thereafter to make his grave.

" I have seen as great a marvel," said Cloudeslè,
  " As between this and prime,
He that maketh this grave for me,
  Himself may lie therein."

" Thou speakest proudly," said the justice,
  " I shall thee hang with my hand : "
Full well that heard his brethren two,
  There still as they did stand.

Then Cloudeslè cast his eyen aside,
  And saw his two brethren stand,
At a corner of the market place,
  With their good bows bent in their hand.

quest, jury.

" I see good comfort," said Cloudeslè,
   " Yet hope I well to fare ;
If I might have my hands at will,
   Right little would I care."

Then spake good Adam Bel,
   To Clym of the Clough so free,
" Brother, see ye mark the justice well,
   Lo yonder ye may him see.

" And at the sheriff shoot I will,
   Strongly with an arrow keen ;
A better shot in merry Carlisle
   This seven year was not seen."

They loosed their arrows both at once,
   Of no man had they dread ;
The one hit the justice, the other the sheriff,
   That both their sides gan bleed.

All men voided, that them stood nigh,
   When the justice fell down to the ground,
And the sheriff fell nigh him by,
   Either had had his death's wound.

All the citizens fast gan fly,
   They durst no longer abide ;
Then lightly they loosed Cloudeslè,
   When he with ropes lay tied.

William stert to an officer of the town,
   His axe out of his hand he wrong,
On each side he smote them down,
   Him thought he tarried all too long.

William said to his brethren two,
   " This day let us together live and die ;
If ever you have need as I have now,
   The same shall you find by me."

They shot so well in that tide,
   For their strings were of silk full sure,
That they kept the streets on every side:
   That battle did long endure.

They fought together as brethren true,
   Like hardy men and bold ;
Many a man to the ground they threw,
   And many a heart made cold.

But when their arrows were all gone,
   Men pressed on them full fast ;
They drew their swords then anon,
   And their bows from them cast.

They went lightly on their way,
   With swords and bucklers round ;
By that it was the middle of the day,
   They had made many a wound.

stert, rushed.   *wrong*, wrung.   *sure*, trusty.

There was many an out-horn in Carlisle blowen,
　And the bells backward did they ring ;
Many a woman said alas,
　And many their hands did wring.

The mayor of Carlisle forth come was,
　And with him a full great rout ;
These three yeomen dread him full sore,
　For of their lives they stood in great doubt.

The mayor came armed a full great pace,
　With a pollaxe in his hand ;
Many a strong man with him was,
　There in that stour to stand.

The mayor smote at Cloudeslè with his bill,
　His buckler he burst in two ;
Full many a yeoman with great ill,
　" Alas, treason ! " they cried for woe.
" Keep we the gates fast," they bad,
　" That these traitors thereout not go."

But all for nought was that they wrought,
　For so fast they down were laid,
Till they all three, that so manfully fought,
　Were gotten without at a braid.

" Have here your keys," said Adam Bel,
　" Mine office I here forsake ;
If you do by my counsèl,
　A new porter do ye make."

　　　　stour, battle.　　　*at a braid*, in a moment.

I

He threw the keys there at their heads,
    And bad them evil to thrive,
And all that letteth any good yeoman
    To come and comfort his wife.

Thus be these good yeomen gone to the wood,
    As light as leaf on lind ;
They laugh and be merry in their mood,
    Their enemies were far behind.

When they came to English wood,
    Under the trysty tree,
There they found bows full good,
    And arrows full great plenty.

"So God me help," said Adam Bel,
    And Clym of the Clough so free,
"I would we were now in merry Carlisle,
    Before that fair meany."

They set them down and made good cheer,
    And eat and drank full well :
Here is a fit of these wight young men,
    And another I shall you tell.

letteth, hindereth.　　　　lind, tree.
trysty tree, trysting tree.　　meany, company.

[THE THIRD FIT.]

As they sat in English-wood,
  Under their trysty tree,
Them thought they heard a woman weep,
  But her they might not see.

Sore then sighed the fair Alice,
  And said, " Alas that ever I saw this day !
For now is my dear husband slain,
  Alas and well a way !

" Might I have spoken with his dear brethren,
  Or with either of them twain,
[To let them know what him befell]
  My heart were out of pain ! "

Cloudeslè walked a little beside,
  And looked under the greenwood lind ;
He was ware of his wife and children three,
  Full woe in heart and mind.

" Welcome, wife," then said William,
  " Under this trysty tree ;
I had weened yesterday, by sweet saint John,
  Thou should me never have see."

" Now well is me," she said, " that ye be here,
  My heart is out of woe : "
" Dame," he said, " be merry and glad,
  And thank my brethren two."

" Hereof to speak," said Adam Bel,
    " I-wis it is no boot ;
The meat that we must sup withal
    It runneth yet fast on foot."

Then went they down into a laund,
    These noble archers all three,
Each of them slew a hart of grice,
    The best they could there see.

" Have here the best, Alice, my wife,"
    Said William of Cloudeslè,
" Because ye so boldly stood by me,
    When I was slain full nigh."

Then went they to supper,
    With such meat as they had,
And thanked God of their fortune ;
    They were both merry and glad.

        laund, glade.   *grice,* grey.

And when they had supped well,
  Certain without any lease,
Cloudeslè said, " We will to our king,
  To get us a charter of peace.

" Alice shall be at sojourning,
  In a nunnery here beside ;
My two sons shall with her go,
  And there they shall abide.

" Mine eldest son shall go with me,
  For him have I no care,
And he shall bring you word again
  How that we do fare."

Thus be these yeomen to London gone,
  As fast as they might hie,
Till they came to the king's palace,
  Where they would needs be.

And when they came to the king's court,
  Unto the palace gate,
Of no man would they aske no leave,
  But boldly went in thereat.

They pressed prestly into the hall,
  Of no man had they dread ;
The porter came after and did them call,
  And with them began to chide.

lease, lies.   *prestly*, quickly.

The usher said, " Yeomen, what would ye have ?
　　I pray you tell me ;
You might thus make officers shent :
　　Good sirs, of whence be ye ?"

" Sir, we be outlaws of the forest,
　　Certain without any lease,
And hither we be come to our king,
　　To get us a charter of peace."

And when they came before the king,
　　As it was the law of the land,
They kneeled down without letting,
　　And each held up his hand.

They said, " Lord, we beseech thee here,
　　That ye will grant us grace,
For we have slain your fat fallow deer,
　　In many a sundry place."

" What be your names ?" then said our king,
　　" Anon that you tell me :"
They said, " Adam Bel, Clym of the Clough,
　　And William of Cloudeslè."

" Be ye those thieves," then said our king,
　　" That men have told of to me ?
Here to God I make a vow,
　　Ye shall be hanged all three.

　　　　　shent. disgraced.

Ye shall be dead without mercy,
  As I am king of this land."
He commanded his officers everyone
  Fast on them to lay hand.

There they took these good yeomen,
  And arrested them all three :
" So may I thrive," said Adam Bel,
  " This game liketh not me.

" But, good lord, we beseech you now,
  That you grant us grace,
Insomuch as we be to you comen,
  Or else that we may fro you pass,

" With such weapons as we have here,
  Till we be out of your place ;
And if we live this hundreth year,
  We will ask you no grace."

" Ye speak proudly," said the king,
  " Ye shall be hanged all three : "
" That were great pity," then said the queen,
  " If any grace might be.

" My lord, when I came first into this land,
  To be your wedded wife,
The first boon that I would ask,
  Ye would grant it me belife ;

belife, at once.

" And I asked never none till now,
  Therefore, good lord, grant it me."
" Now ask it, madam," said the king,
  " And granted shall it be."

" Then, my good lord, I you beseech,
  These yeomen grant ye me : "
" Madam, ye might have asked a boon
  That should have been worth them all three.

" Ye might have asked towers and towns,
  Parks and forests plenty."
" None so pleasant to me pay," she said,
  " Nor none so lief to me."

" Madam, sith it is your desire,
  Your asking granted shall be ;
But I had liefer have given you
  Good market towns three."

The queen was a glad woman,
  And said, " Lord, gramercy ;
I dare undertake for them,
  That true men shall they be.

" But, good lord, speak some merry word,
  That comfort they may see."
" I grant you grace," then said our king,
  " Wash, fellows, and to meat go ye."

They had not setten but a while,
  Certain without leasing,
There came messengers out of the north,
  With letters to our king.

And when they came before the king,
  They kneeled down upon their knee,
And said, " Lord, your officers greet you well,
  Of Carlisle in the north countrè."

" How fares my justice," said the king,
  "And my sheriff also?"
" Sir, they be slain, without leasing,
  And many an officer moe."

" Who hath them slain?" said the king,
  " Anon thou tell me:"
" Adam Bel, and Clym of the Clough,
  And William of Cloudeslè."

" Alas for ruth!" then said our king,
  " My heart is wondrous sore;
I had liefer than a thousand pound,
  I had known of this before.

" For I have granted them grace,
  And that forthinketh me,
But had I known all this before,
  They had been hanged all three."

leasing, lying.   *forthinketh*, repenteth

The king opened the letter anon,
  Himself he read it thro,
And found how these three outlaws had slain
  Three hundred men and moe.

First the justice and the sheriff,
  And the mayor of Carlisle town ;
Of all the constables and catchpolls
  Alive were left not one.

The bailiffs and the beadle both,
  And the sergeants of the law,
And forty fosters of the fee,
  These outlaws had yslaw,

And broke his parks, and slain his deer ;
  Over all they chose the best ;
So perilous outlaws as they were,
  Walked not by east nor west.

When the king this letter had read,
  In his heart he sighed sore ;
" Take up the table anon," he bad,
  " For I may eat no more."

The king called his best archers,
  To the butts with him to go ;
" I will see these fellows shoot," he said,
  " In the north have wrought this woe."

catchpolls, bumbailiffs.   *fosters*, foresters.
of the fee, in the pay of the king.   *yslaw*, slain

The king's bowmen busk them blithe,
  And the queen's archers also,
So did these three wight yeomèn,
  With them they thought to go.

There twice or thrice they shot about,
  For to essay their hand ;
There was no shot these yeomen shot,
  That any prick might them stand.

Then spake William of Cloudeslè,
  " By Him that for me died,
I hold him never no good archer
  That shooteth at butts so wide."

" Whereat ? " then said our king,
  " I pray thee tell me : "
" At such a butt, sir," he said,
  " As men use in my countre."

William went into a field,
  And his two brethren with him,
There they set up two hazel rods,
  Twenty score paces between.

" I hold him an archer," said Cloudeslè,
  " That yonder wand cleaveth in two :
" Here is none such," said the king,
  " Nor none that can so do."

busk, make ready.   *prick*, peg in target

"I shall essay, sir," said Cloudeslè,
　"Or that I farther go :"
Cloudeslè, with a bearing arrow,
　Clave the wand in two.

"Thou art the best archer," then said the
　　king,
　"Forsooth that ever I see :"
"And yet for your love," said William,
　"I will do more maistry.

"I have a son is seven year old,
　He is to me full dear ;
I will him tie to a stake,
　All shall see that be here ;

"And lay an apple upon his head,
　And go six score paces him fro,
And I myself, with a broad arrow,
　Shall cleave the apple in two."

"Now haste thee," then said the king,
　"By Him that died on a tree ;
But if thou do not as thou hast said,
　Hanged shalt thou be.

"And thou touch his head or gown,
　In sight that men may see,
By all the saints that be in heaven,
　I shall hang you all three."

maistry, mastery.

"That I have promised," said William,
  "I will it never forsake ;"
And there even before the king,
  In the earth he drove a stake,

And bound thereto his eldest son,
  And bad him stand still thereat,
And turned the child's face fro him,
  Because he should not start.

An apple upon his head he set,
  And then his bow he bent ;
Six score paces they were out met,
  And thither Cloudeslè went.

There he drew out a fair broad arrow,
  His bow was great and long,
He set that arrow in his bow,
  That was both stiff and strong.

He prayed the people that was there,
  That they would still stand,
"For he that shooteth for such a wager,
  Behoveth a stedfast hand."

Much people prayed for Cloudeslè,
  That his life saved might be,
And when he made him ready to shoot,
  There was many a weeping eye.

met, meted, measured.

Thus Cloudeslè cleft the apple in two,
   That many a man might see ;
" Over God's forbode," said the king,
   " That thou shoot at me !

" I give thee xviii. pence a day,
   And my bow shalt thou bear,
And over all the north countre,
   I make thee chief rider."

" And I give thee xvii. pence a day," said
    the queen,
   " By God and by my fay ;
Come fetch thy payment when thou wilt,
   No man shall say thee nay.

" William, I make thee a gentleman,
   Of clothing and of fee,
And thy two brethren yeomen of my chamber,
   For they are so seemly to see.

" Your son, for he is tender of age,
   Of my wine-cellar shall he be,
And when he cometh to man's estate,
   Better avaunced shall he be.

" And, William, bring me your wife," said
    the queen,
   " Me longeth her sore to see ;
She shall be my chief gentlewoman,
   To govern my nursery."

fay, faith.
Over God's forbode, on God's prohibition, *i.e.* God forbid.

The yeomen thanketh them full courteously,
   And said, " To some bishop will we wend,
Of all the sins that we have done
   To be assoiled at his hand."

So forth be gone these good yeomen,
   As fast as they might hie,
And after came and dwelled with the king,
   And died good men all three.

Thus endeth the lives of these good yeomen,
   God send them eternal bliss,
And all that with hand bow shooteth,
   That of heaven may never miss.

assoiled, absolved.

The

Brave

Earl

Brand

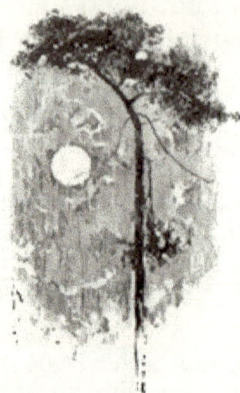

O DID you ever hear o' brave Earl Bran?
　　Ay lally, o lilly lally!
He courted the king's daughter of fair England,
　　All i' the night sae early.

She was scarcely fifteen years of age,
'Till sae boldly she came to his bed-side.

" O, Earl Bran, fain wad I see
A pack of hounds let loose on the lea."

" O lady, I have no steeds but one,
And thou shalt ride, and I will run."

" O Earl Bran, my father has two,
And thou shalt have the best of them a'."

They have ridden o'er moss and moor,
And they met neither rich nor poor,

Until they met with old Carl Hood,
He comes for ill, but never for good.

" Earl Bran, if ye love me,
Seize this old carl, and gar him die."

" O lady fair, it wad be sair,
To slay an old man that has grey hair.

" O lady fair, I'll no do sae,
I'll gie him a pound, and let him gae."

" O where hae ye ridden this lee lang day,
And where hae ye stolen this lady away ? "

" I have not ridden this lee lang day,
Nor yet have I stolen this lady away.

" She is my only, my sick sister,
Whom I have brought from Winchester."

" If she be sick, and like to dead,
Why wears she the ribbon sae red ?

" If she be sick, and like to die,
Then why wears she the gold on high ? "

Then he came to this lady's gate,
Sae rudely as he rapped at it.

" O where's the lady of this ha' ? "
" She's out with her maids to play at the ba'."

K

" Ha, ha, ha ! ye are a' mista'en ;
Gae count your maidens o'er again.

" I saw her far beyond the moor,
Away to be the Earl o' Bran's whore."

The father armed fifteen of his best men,
To bring his daughter back again.

O'er her left shoulder the lady looked then ;
" O Earl Bran, we both are ta'en."

" If they come on me ane by ane,
You may stand by and see them slain."

" But if they come on me one and all,
You may stand by and see me fall."

They have come on him ane by ane,
And he has killed them all but ane.

And that ane came behind his back,
And he's gi'en him a deadly whack.

But for a' sae wounded as Earl Bran was,
He has set his lady on her horse.

They rode till they came to the water o' Doune,
And then he alighted to wash his wounds.

"O Earl Bran, I see your heart's blood!"
"'Tis but the gleat o' my scarlet hood."

They rode till they came to his mother's gate,
And sae rudely as he rapped at it.

"O my son's slain, my son's put down,
And a' for the sake of an English loon."

gleat, gleam.

"O say not sae, my dear mother,
But marry her to my youngest brother.

"This has not been the death o' ane,
But it's been that of fair seventeen."

The Nutbrown Maid

"BE it right or wrong, these men among
  On women do complain,
Affirming this, how that it is
  A labour spent in vain
To love them weel, for never a deal
  They love a man again :
For let a man do what he can
  Their favour to attain,
Yet if a new do them pursue,
  Their first true lover than
Laboureth for nought, and from her thought
  He is a banished man."

deal, bit.   *than*, then.

" I say not nay, but that all day
    It is both writ and said,
That woman's faith is, as who saith,
    All utterly decayed :
But nevertheless, right good witness
    In this case might be laid,
That they love true, and continue,—
    Record THE NUTBROWN MAID ;
Which from her love, when her to prove
    He came to make his moan,
Would not depart, for in her heart
    She loved but him alone."

" Then between us let us discuss
    What was all the mannér
Between them two ; we will also
    Tell all the pain and fear
That she was in ; now I begin,
    See that ye me answér :
Wherefore [all] ye that present be,
    I pray you give an ear.
I am the knight, I come by night,
    As secret as I can,
Saying ' Alas ! thus standeth the case,
    I am a banished man ! ' "

" And I your will for to fulfill
    In this will not refuse,
Trusting to shew, in words few,
    That men have an ill use,

To their own shame, women to blame,
  And causeless them accuse :
Therefore to you I answer now,
  All women to excuse,
' Mine own heart dear, with you what cheer ?
  I pray you tell anon :
For in my mind, of all mankind
  I love but you alone.' "

" It standeth so : a deed is do
  Whereof much harm shall grow.
My destiny is for to die
  A shameful death, I trow,
Or else to flee,—the one must be :
  None other way I know,
But to withdraw as an outlaw,
  And take me to my bow.
Wherefore, adieu, my own heart true,
  None other red I can ;
For I must to the green wood go,
  Alone, a banished man."

" O Lord, what is this worldés bliss
  That changeth as the moon !
My summer's day in lusty May
  Is darked before the noon.
I hear you say Farewell : nay, nay,
  We depart not so soon.
Why say ye so ? Whither will ye go ?
  Alas, what have ye done ?

red, plan.   *darked*, darkened.

All my welfare to sorrow and care
   Should change, if ye were gone :
For in my mind, of all mankind
   I love but you alone."

" I can believe it shall you grieve,
   And somewhat you distrain ;
But afterward your painés hard,
   Within a day or twain,
Shall soon aslake, and ye shall take
   Comfort to you again.
Why should ye nought ? for, to make thought
   Your labour were in vain :
And thus I do, and pray you, too,
   As heartily as I can :
For I must to the green wood go,
   Alone, a banished man."

" Now sith that ye have shewed to me
   The secret of your mind,
I shall be plain to you again,
   Like as ye shall me find :
Sith it is so that ye will go,
   I will not leave behind ;
Shall never be said the Nutbrown Maid
   Was to her love unkind.
Make you ready, for so am I,
   Although it were anon ;
For in my mind, of all mankind
   I love but you alone."

" Yet I you rede to take good heed
　　What men will think and say ;
Of young and old it shall be told,
　　That ye be gone away
Your wanton will for to fulfil,
　　In green wood you to play ;
And that ye might from your delight
　　No longer make delay.
Rather than ye should thus for me
　　Be called an ill woman,
Yet would I to the green wood go
　　Alone, a banished man."

" Though it be sung of old and young
　　That I should be to blame,
Theirs be the charge that speak so large
　　In hurting of my name.
For I will prove that faithful love
　　It is devoid of shame,
In your distress and heaviness,
　　To part with you the same ;
And sure all tho that do not so,
　　True lovers are they none ;
But in my mind, of all mankind
　　I love but you alone."

" I counsel yow remember how
　　It is no maiden's law,
Nothing to doubt, but to renne out
　　To wood with an outlaw.

　　tho, those.　　　　　　　　　　*renne*, run.

For ye must there in your hand bear
    A bow to bear and draw,
And as a thief thus must ye live,
    Ever in dread and awe ;
By which to yow great harm might grow ;—
    Yet had I liefer than
That I had to the greenwood go
    Alone, a banished man."

" I think not nay ; but, as ye say,
    It is no maiden's lore ;
But love may make me for your sake,
    As ye have said before,
To come on foot, to hunt and shoot
    To get us meat and store ;
For so that I your company
    May have, I ask no more ;
From which to part, it maketh mine heart
    As cold as any stone :
For in my mind, of all mankind
    I love but you alone."

" For an outlaw this is the law,
    That men him take and bind,
Without pity hanged to be,
    And waver with the wind.
If I had need, as God forbid,
    What rescue could ye find ?
For sooth, I trow, you and your bow
    Should draw for fear behind :

And no merveil ; for little avail
   Were in your counsel than ;
Wherefore I to the wood will go
   Alone, a banished man."

" Full well know ye that women be
   Full feeble for to fight ;
No womanhead is it indeed,
   To be bold as a knight.
Yet in such fear if that ye were,
   Among enemies day and night,
I would withstand, with bow in hand,
   To grieve them as I might,
And you to save, as women have,
   From death many one :
For in my mind, of all mankind
   I love but you alone."

" Yet take good heed ; for ever I dread
   That ye could not sustain
The thorny ways, the deep vallies,
   The snow, the frost, the rain,
The cold, the heat ; for, dry or wet,
   We must lodge on the plain ;
And us above none other rove
   But a brake bush or twain ;
Which soon should grieve you, I believe,
   And ye would gladly than
That I had to the greenwood go
   Alone, a banished man."

than, then.   *rove*, roof.

"Sith I have here been partinere
  With you of joy and bliss,
I must also part of your woe
  Endure, as reason is ;
Yet am I sure of one pleasure,
  And shortly, it is this ;
That where ye be, meseemth, perdé,
  I could not fare amiss.
Without more speech, I you beseech
  That we were soon agone ;
For in my mind, of all mankind
  I love but you alone."

"If ye go thither, ye must consider,
  When ye have lust to dine,
There shall no meat be for to get,
  Nor drink, beer, ale, ne wine ;
Ne sheetés clean to lie between,
  Made of thread and twine :
None other house but leaves and boughs
  To cover your head and mine.
Lo, mine heart sweet, this ill diet
  Should make you pale and wan :
Wherefore I to the wood will go
  Alone, a banished man."

"Among the wild deer such an archer
  As men say that ye be
Ne may not fail of good vitail,
  Where is so great plenty ;

partinere, partner.   vitail, victual

And water clear of the river
  Shall be full sweet to me,
With which in hele I shall right weel
  Endure, as ye shall see :
And ere we go, a bed or two
  I can provide anon ;
For in my mind, of all mankind
  I love but you alone."

" Lo, yet before, ye must do more,
  If ye will go with me,
As cut your hair up by your ear,
  Your kirtle by the knee ;
With bow in hand, for to withstand
  Your enemies, if need be ;
And this same night, before daylight,
  To woodward will I flee ;
And [if] ye will all this fulfill,
  Do it shortly as ye can :
Else will I to the greenwood go
  Alone, a banished man."

" I shall as now do more for you
  Than longeth to womanhood,
To short my hair, a bow to bear,
  To shoot in time of need :
O my sweet mother, before all other,
  For you have I most dread !
But now, adieu ! I must ensue
  Where fortune doth me lead.

hele, health.

All this make ye ; now let us flee ;
  The day comes fast upon ;
For in my mind, of all mankind
  I love but you alone."

" Nay, nay, not so ; ye shall not go ;
  And I shall tell you why ;
Your appetite is to be light
  Of love, I well espy :
For right as ye have said to me,
  In like wise, hardily,
Ye would answer, who so ever it were,
  In way of company.
It is said of old, soon hot, soon cold,
  And so is a woman ;
Wherefore I to the wood will go
  Alone, a banished man."

" If ye take heed, it is no need
  Such words to say by me ;
For oft ye prayed, and long assayed,
  Or I you loved, perdé.
And though that I of ancestry
  A baron's daughter be,
Yet have you proved how I you loved,
  A squire of low degree ;
And ever shall, what so befall,
  To die therefore anon ;
For in my mind, of all mankind
  I love but you alone."

" A baron's child to be beguiled,
  It were a cursed deed !
To be fellow with an outlaw,
  Almighty God forbid !
Yet better were the poor squire
  Alone to forest yede,
Than ye shall say another day,
  That by [my] wicked deed
Ye were betrayed ; wherefore, good maid,
  The best red that I can
Is that I to the green wood go
  Alone, a banished man."

" Whatsoever befall, I never shall
  Of this thing you upbraid ;
But if ye go, and leave me so,
  Then have ye me betrayed.
Remember you weel, how that ye deal,
  For if ye, as ye said,
Be so unkind to leave behind
  Your love, the Nutbrown Maid,
Trust me truly, that I shall die,
  Soon after ye be gone ;
For in my mind, of all mankind
  I love but you alone."

" If that ye went, ye should repent,
  For in the forest now
I have purveyed me of a maid
  Whom I love more than you :

yede, went.   *red*, advice.

Another fairer than ever ye were,
　I dare it well avow ;
And of you both each should be wroth
　With other, as I trow.
It were mine ease to live in peace ;
　So will I, if I can ;
Wherefore I to the wood will go
　Alone, a banished man."

" Though in the wood I understood
　Ye had a paramour,
All this may nought remove my thought,
　But that I will be your ;
And she shall find me soft and kind
　And courteous every hour,
Glad to fulfill all that she will
　Command me to my power ;
For had ye, lo'e, an hundred moe
　Yet would I be that one.
For in my mind, of all mankind
　I love but you alone."

" Mine own dear love, I see the prove
　That ye be kind and true ;
Of maid and wife, in all my life,
　The best that ever I knew.
Be merry and glad, be no more sad,
　The case is changed new ;
For it were ruth that for your truth
　You should have cause to rue.
　　　　　lo'e, love.

Be not dismayed : whatsoever I said
  To you when I began,
I will not to the green wood go ;
  I am no banished man."

" This tidings be more glad to me
  Than to be made a queen,
If I were sure they should endure,
  But it is often seen,
When men will break promise, they speak
  The wordés on the spleen.
Ye shape some wile me to beguile,
  And steal fro me, I ween ;
Then were the case worse than it was,
  And I more woe-begone ;
For in my mind, of all mankind
  I love but you alone."

" Ye shall not need further to dread :
  I will not disparage
You, God defend ! sith you descend
  Of so great a lineage.
Now understand, to Westmoreland,
  Which is my heritage,
I will you bring, and with a ring,
  By way of marriage,
I will you take, and lady make,
  As shortly as I can :
Thus have ye won an earlés son,
  And not a banished man."

Here may ye see that women be
   In love meek, kind, and stable :
Let never man reprove them than,
   Or call them variable ;
But rather pray God, that we may
   To them be comfortable,
Which sometime proveth such as loveth,
   If they be charitable ;
For sith men would that women should
   Be meek to them each one,
Much more ought they to God obey,
   And serve but Him alone.

L

Robin

Hood

and

Guy

of

Gisborne

ĕ

WHEN shaws been sheen, and shrads full fair,
    And leaves both large and long,'
It is merry walking in the fair forrèst,
    To hear the small bird's song.

The woodweel sang, and would not cease,
    Among the leaves o' line;
And it is by two wight yeomen,
    By dear God, that I mean.[1]

shaws, wood.   *sheen,* bright.
shrad, an opening in a wood.   *line,* tree.

[1] The lost stanza probably states that Robin Hood is having
a dream.

.   .   .   .   .   .

" Methought they did me beat and bind,
    And took my bow me fro ;
If I be Robin alive in this land,
    I'll be wroken on them two."

" Swevens are swift, master," quoth John,
    " As the wind that blows o'er a hill ;
For if it be never so loud this night,
    To-morrow it may be still."

" Busk ye, boun ye, my merry men all,
    For John shall go with me,
For I'll go seek yond wight yeomèn,
    In greenwood where they be."

They cast on their gowns of green,
    A shooting gone are they ;
Until they came to the merry greenwood,
    Where they had gladdest be ;
There were they ware of [a] wight yeomàn,
    His body leaned to a tree.

A sword and a dagger he wore by his side,
    Had been many a man's bane ;
And he was clad in his capull hide,
    Top and tail and mane.

wroken, revenged.	*swevens*, dreams.
boun, make ready.	*capull*, horse.

"Stand you still, master," quoth Little John,
  "Under this trusty tree,
And I will go to yond wight yeomàn,
  To know his meaning truly."

"Ah! John, by me thou sets no store,
  And that's a farley thing :
How oft send I my men before,
  And tarry myself behind ?

"It is no cunning a knave to ken,
  And a man but hear him speak ;
And it were not for bursting of my bow,
  John, I would thy head break."

But often words they breeden bale,
  That parted Robin and John ;
John is gone to Barnesdale ;
  The gates he knows each one.

And when he came to Barnesdale,
  Great heaviness there he had,
He found two of his own fellòws,
  Were slain both in a slade.

And Scarlet a-foot flying was
  Over stocks and stone, ·
For the sheriff with seven score men
  Fast after him is gone.

farley, strange.   *bale*, mischief or sorrow.   *slade*, valley.

" Yet one shot I'll shoot," says Little John,
    " With Christ his might and main ;
I'll make yond fellow that flies so fast,
    To be both glad and fain."

John bent up a good yew bow,
    And fettled him to shoot :
The bow was made of a tender bough,
    And fell down to his foot.

" Woe worth thee, wicked wood," said Little
        John,
    " That ere thou grew on a tree !
For this day thou art my bale,
    My boot when thou should be."

This shot it was but loosely shot,
    The arrow flew in vain,
And it met one of the sheriff's men,
    Good William a Trent was slain.

It had been better for William a Trent
    To have been upon a gallow,
Than for to lie in the greenwood
    There slain with an arrow.

And it is said, when men be met
    Six can do more than three,
And they have ta'en Little John,
    And bound him fast to a tree.
                fettled. made ready.

" Thou shalt be drawn by dale and down,"
　　quoth the sheriff,
　" And hanged high on a hill ; "
" But thou may fail," quoth John,
　" If it be Christ's own will."

Let us leave talking of Little John,
　For he is bound fast to a tree,
And talk of Guy and Robin Hood,
　In the green wood where they be.

How these two yeomen together they met,
　Under the leaves of line,
To see what merchandise they made,
　Even at that same time.

" Good morrow, good fellow," quoth Sir Guy,
　" Good morrow, good fellow," quoth he :
" Methinks by this bow thou bears in thy hand,
　A good archer thou seems to be.

" I am wilful of my way," quoth Sir Guy,
　" And of my morning tide : "
"I'll lead thee through the wood,"quoth Robin,
　" Good fellow, I'll be thy guide."

" I seek an outlaw," quoth Sir Guy,
　" Men call him Robin Hood :
I'd rather meet with him upon a day,
　Than forty pound of gold."

line, tree.

" If you two met, it would be seen whether
    were better,
  Afore ye did part away ;
Let us some other pastime find,
  Good fellow, I thee pray.

" Let us some masteries make,
  And we will walk in the woods even ;
We may chance meet with Robin Hood
  Here at some unset steven."

They cut them down two summer shrogs,
  Which grew both under a briar,
And set them threescore rood in twin,
  To shoot the pricks full near.

" Lead on, good fellow," said Sir Guy,
  " Lead on, I do bid thee ; "
" Nay, by my faith," quoth Robin Hood,
  " The leader thou shalt be."

The first good shot that Robin led
  Did not shoot an inch the prick fro' ;
Guy was an archer good enough,
  But he could ne'er shoot so.

unset steven, unappointed time.
shrogs, shrubs.
in twin, apart.

The second shot Sir Guy shot,
 He shot within the garlànd ;
But Robin Hood shot it better than he,
 For he clove the good prick-wand.

" God's blessing on thy heart," says Guy,
 " Good fellow, thy shooting is good ;
For an thy heart be as good as thy hand
 Thou were better then Robin Hood.

" Tell me thy name, good fellow," quoth Guy,
 " Under the leaves of line ; "
" Nay, by my faith," quoth good Robin,
 " Till thou have told me thine."

" I dwell by dale and down," quoth Guy,
 " And I have done many a cursed turn ;
And he that calls me by my right name,
 Calls me Guy of good Gisbòrne."

" My dwelling is in the wood," says Robin,
 " By thee I set right nought :
I am Robin Hood of Barnésdale,
 A fellow thou has long sought."

He that had neither been a kith nor kin
 Might have seen a full fair fight,
To see how together these yeomen went
 With blades both brown and bright :

To have seen how these yeomen together
        fought
Two hours of a summers day,
It was neither Guy nor Robin Hood
    That fettled them to fly away.

Robin was reachless on a root,
    And stumbled at that tide ;
And Guy was quick and nimble withal,
    And hit him o'er the left side.

" Ah, dear Lady," said Robin Hood,
    " Thou art both mother and may ;
I think it was never man's destiny
    To die before his day."   ·

Robin thought on our lady dear,
    And soon leapt up again,
And thus he came with an awkward stroke,
    Good Sir Guy he hath slain.

He took Sir Guy's head by the hair,
    And sticked it on his bow's end :
" Thou hast been traitor all thy life,
    Which thing must have an end."

Robin pulled forth an Irish knife,
 · And nicked Sir Guy in the face,
That he was never on woman born
    Could tell who Sir Guy was.

                reachless, reckless.

Says, " Lie there, lie there, good Sir Guy,
   And with me be not wroth ;
If thou have had the worse strokes at my hand,
   Thou shalt have the better cloth."

Robin did off his gown of green,
   [On] Sir Guy he did it throw,
And he put on that capull hide,
   That clad him top to toe.

" The bow, the arrows, and little horn,
   And with me now I'll bear ;
For I will go to Barnésdale,
   To see how my men do fare."

Robin Hood set Guy's horn to his mouth,
   And a loud blast in it he did blow :
That beheard the sheriff of Nottingham,
   As he leaned under a lowe.

" Hearken, hearken," said the sheriff,
   " I heard no tidings but good,
For yonder I hear Sir Guy's horn blow,
   For he hath slain Robin Hood.

" For yonder I hear Sir Guy's horn blow,
   It blows so well in tide,
For yonder comes that wight yeomàn,
   Clad in his capull hide.

        lowe, small hill.

"Come hither, thou good Sir Guy,
　Ask of me what thou wilt : "
"I'll have none of thy gold," says Robin Hood,
　"Nor I'll none of it have.

"But now I have slain the master," he said,
　"Let me go strike the knave ;
This is all the reward I ask,
　Nor no other will I have."

"Thou art a madman," said the sheriff,
　"Thou shouldest have had a knight's fee ;
Seeing thy asking hath been so bad,
　Well granted it shall be."

But Little John heard his master speak,
　Well he knew that was his steven ;
"Now shall I be loosed," quoth Little John,
　"With Christ's might in heaven."

But Robin he hied him towards Little John,
　He thought he would loose him belive :
The sheriff and all his company
　Fast after him did drive.

"Stand aback, stand aback," said Robin,
　"Why draw you me so near ?
It was never the use in our country,
　One's shrift another should hear."

steven, voice.　　　*belive*, quickly.

But Robin pulled forth an Irish knife,
  And loosed John hand and foot,
And gave him Sir Guy's bow in his hand,
  And bade it be his boot.

But John took Guy's bow in his hand,
  His arrows were rusty by the root:
The sheriff saw Little John draw a bow,
  And fettle him to shoot.

Towards his house in Nottingham
  He fled full fast away,
And so did all his company,
  Not one behind did stay.

But he could neither so fast go,
  Nor away so fast run,
But Little John with an arrow broad
  Did cleave his heart in twin.

─·≑═╞═╡≡:·─

≈ Old Robin
of Portingale ≈

God let never so old a man
  Marry so young a wife,
As did old Robin of Portingale;
  He may rue all the days of his life.

        fettle, make ready.

For the mayor's daughter of Lynn, God wot,
   He chose her to his wife,
And thought to have lived in quietness,
   With her all the days of his life.

They had not in their wed-bed laid,
   Scarcely were both on sleep,
But up she rose, and forth she goes,
   To Sir Gyles, and fast can weep.

Says, " Sleep you, wake you, fair Sir Gyles ?
   Or be you not within ?
[Sleep you, wake you, fair Sir Gyles,
   Arise and let me in."]

" But I am waking, sweet," he said,
   " Lady, what is your will ? "
" I have unbethought me of a wile
   How my wed lord we shall spill.

" Four and twenty knights," she says,
   " That dwells about this town,
E'en four and twenty of my next cousins
   Will help to ding him down."

With that beheard his little footpage,
   As he was watering his master's steed ;
[And for his master's sad peril]
   His very heart did bleed.

ding, knock.

He mourned, sighed, and wept full sore ;
    I swear by the holy rood,
The tears he for his master wept
    Were blend water and blood.

With that beheard his dear master
    As [he] in his garden sat :
Says, " Ever alack, my little page,
    What causes thee to weep ?

" Hath any one done to thee wrong,
    Any of thy fellows here ?
Or is any of thy good friends dead,
    Which makes thee shed such tears ?

" Or, if it be my head cook's-man,
    Grieved again he shall be :
Nor no man within my house
    Shall do wrong unto thee."

" But it is not your head cook's-man,
    Nor none of his degree :
But, for to-morrow ere it be noon
    You are deemed to die :

" And of that thank your head steward,
    And after, your gay lady."
" If it be true, my little foot-page,
    I'll make thee heir of all my land."

deemed, doomed.

" If it be not true, my dear master,
  God let me never the : "
" If it be not true, thou little foot-page,
  A dead corse shalt thou be."

He called down his head cook's-man,
  Cook in kitchen supper to dress :
" All and anon, my dear master,
  Anon at your request."

.   .   .   .   .

" And call you down my fair lady
  This night to sup with me."

And down then came that fair lady,
  Was clad all in purple and pall :
The rings that were upon her fingers,
  Cast light thorow the hall.

" What is your will, my own wed lord ?
  What is your will with me ? "
" I am sick, fair lady,
  Sore sick and like to die."

" But and you be sick, my own wed lord,
  So sore it grieveth me :
But my five maidens and myself
  Will go and make your bed.

" And at the wakening of your first sleep,
  You shall have a hot drink made ;
And at the wakening of your next sleep
  Your sorrows will have a slake."

the, prosper.

He put a silk coat on his back,
   Was thirteen inches fold ;
And put a steel cap upon his head,
   Was gilded with good red gold.

And he laid a bright brown sword by his side,
   And another at his feet :
And full well knew old Robin then   ·
   Whether he should wake or sleep.

And about the middle time of the night,
   Came twenty-four good knights ;
Sir Gyles he was the foremost man,
   So well he knew that gin.

Old Robin with a bright brown sword,
   Sir Gyles' head he did win ;
So did he all those twenty-four
   Never a one went quick out [agen].

None but one little foot-page,
   Crept forth at a window of stone ;
And he had two arms when he came in,
   And [when he went out he had none].

Up then came that lady gay,
   With torches burning bright ;
She thought to have brought Sir Gyles a drink,
   But she found her own wed knight.

gin, trick.

And the first thing that this lady stumbled upon
   Was of Sir Gyles his foot ;
Says, " Ever alack, and woe is me !
   Here lies my sweet heart-root."

And the second thing that this lady stumbled on
   Was of Sir Gyles his head ;
Says, " Ever alack, and woe is me !
   Here lies my true love dead."

He cut the paps beside her breast,
   And bade her wish her will ;
And he cut the ears beside her head
   And bade her wish on still.

Mickle is the man's blood I have spent,
   To do thee and me some good ;
Says, " Ever alack, my fair lady,
   I think that I was wood ! "

He called then up his little foot-page,
   And made him heir of all his land ;
And he shope the cross on his right shoulder,
   Of the white flesh and the red,
And he went him into the holy land,
   Whereas Christ was quick and dead.

shope, shaped, cut.   *wood*, mad.

M

Captain
Car,
or
Edom
o'
Gordon.

IT befell at Martinmas
  When weather waxed cold,
Captain Car said to his men,
  "We must go take a hold."

Sick, sick, and too-too sick,
  And sick and like to die;
The sickest night that ever I abode,
  God Lord have mercy on me.

" Hail, master, and whither you will,
    And whither ye like it best."
" To the castle of Craickernbrough ;
    And there we will take our rest.

" I know where is a gay castle,
    Is builded of lime and stone,
Within there is a gay lady,
    Her lord is ridden and gone."

The lady she leaned on her castle-wall,
    She looked up and down ;
There was she ware of an host of men,
    Come riding to the town.

" See now, my merry men all,
    And see you what I see ;
Yonder I see an host of men,
    I muse who they be."

She thought he had been her wed lord,
    As he comed riding home ;
Then was it traitor Captain Car,
    The lord of Ester-town.

They were no sooner at supper set,
    Then after said the grace,
Or Captain Car and all his men
    Were light about the place.

"Give over this house, thou lady gay,
  And I will make thee a band ;
To-night thou shall lie within my arms,
  To-morrow thou shall heir my land."

Then bespake the eldest son,
  That was both white and red,
"O mother dear, give over your house,
  Or else we shall be dead."

"I will not give over my house," she saith,
  "Not for fear of my life ;
It shall be talked throughout the land,
  The slaughter of a wife.

"Fetch me my pestilet,
  And charge me my gun,
That I may shoot at yonder bloody butcher,
  The lord of Ester-town."

Stiffly upon her wall she stood,
  And let the pellets flee,
But then she missed the bloody butcher,
  And she slew other three.

"[I will] not give over my house," she saith,
  "Neither for lord nor loon,
Nor yet for traitor Captain Car,
  The lord of Ester-town.

  band, bond.   *pestilet*, pistols.

"I desire of Captain Car,
  And all his bloody band,
That he would save my eldest son,
  The heir of all my land."

"Lap him in a sheet," he saith,
  "And let him down to me,
And I shall take him in my arms,
  His warrant shall I be."

The captain said unto himself,
  With speed before the rest ;
He cut his tongue out of his head,
  His heart out of his brest.

He lapt them in a handerchief,
  And knit it of knots three,
And cast them over the castle-wall
  At that gay lady.

"Fie upon thee, Captain Car,
  And all thy bloody band,
For thou hast slain my eldest son,
  The heir of all my land."

Then bespake the youngest son,
  That sat on the nurses knee,
Saith, "Mother gay, give over your house,
  It smouldereth me."

" I would give my gold," she saith,
  " And so I would my fee,
For a blast of the western wind
  To drive the smoke from thee.

" Fie upon thee, John Hamilton,
  That ever I paid thee hire,
For thou hast broken my castle-wall,
  And kindled in the fire."

The lady gat to her close parlor,
  The fire fell about her head ;
She took up her children three,
  Saith, " Babes, we are all dead."

Then bespake the high steward,
  That is of high degree ;
Saith, " Lady gay, you are enclosed,
  Whether ye fight or flee."

Lord Hamilton dreamed in his dream,
  In Carvall where he lay,
His hall was all of fire,
  His lady slain or day.

" Busk and boun, my merry men all,
  Even and go ye with me,
For I dreamed that my hall was on fire
  My lady slain or day."

or day. before day.

He busked him and bouned him,
  And like a worthy knight,
And when he saw his hall burning,
  His heart was no deal light.

He set a trumpet till his mouth,
  He blew as it pleased his grace ;
Twenty score of Hamiltons
  Was light about the place.

" Had I known as much yesternight
  As I do to-day,
Captain Car and all his men
  Should not have gone so quite [away].

" Fie upon thee, Captain Car,
  And all thy bloody band ;
Thou hast slain my lady gay,
  More worth then all thy land.

" If thou had ought any ill will," he saith,
  " Thou should have taken my life,
And have saved my children three,
  All and my lovesome wife."

                    bounnd, prepared.

The Battle ≋
≋ of Otterbourne

It fell about the Lammas tide,
　　When the muir-men win their hay,
The doughty Douglas bouned him to ride
　　Into England, to drive a prey.

He chose the Gordons and the Græmes,
　　With them the Lindsays, light and gay ;
But the Jardines wad not with him ride,
　　And they rue it to this day.

And he has burn'd the dales of Tyne,
　　And part of Bambroughshire ;
And three good towers on Reidswire fells,
　　He left them all on fire.

And he march'd up to Newcastle,
　　And rode it round about ;
"O wha's the lord of this castle,
　　Or wha's the lady o't ? "

But up spake proud Lord Percy then,
　　And O but he spake high !
"I am the lord of this castle,
　　My wife's the lady gay."

　　　　muir, moor.　　　　　*win*, make.

" If thou'rt the lord of this castle,
　　Sae weel it pleases me !
For, ere I cross the Border fells,
　　The tane of us shall die."

He took a lang spear in his hand,
　　Shod with the metal free,
And for to meet the Douglas there,
　　He rode right furiously.

But O how pale his lady look'd,
　　Frae aff the castle wa',
When down before the Scottish spear
　　She saw proud Percy fa'.

" Had we twa been upon the green,
　　And never an eye to see,
I wad hae had you, flesh and fell ;
　　But your sword sall gae wi' me."

" But gae ye up to Otterbourne,
　　And wait there dayés three ;
And if I come not ere three dayés end,
　　A fause knight ca' ye me."

" The Otterbourne's a bonnie burn ;
　　'Tis pleasant there to be ;
But there is nought at Otterbourne,
　　To feed my men and me.

free, precious.

" The deer rins wild on hill and dale,
    The birds fly wild from tree to tree ;
But there is neither bread nor kale,
    To fend my men and me.

" Yet I will stay at Otterbourne,
    Where you shall welcome be ;
And if ye come not at three days end,
    A fause lord I'll ca' thee."

" Thither will I come," proud Percy said,
    " By the might of Our Lady ! "
" There will I bide thee," said the Douglas,
    " My troth I plight to thee."

They lighted high on Otterbourne,
    Upon the bent sae brown ;
They lighted high on Otterbourne,
    And threw their pallions down.

And he that had a bonnie boy,
    Sent out his horse to grass ;
And he that had not a bonnie boy,
    His ain servant he was.

But up then spake a little page,
    Before the peep of dawn—
" O waken ye, waken ye, my good lord,
    For Percy's hard at hand."

kale, broth.	*fend*, keep, support.
bent, field.	*pallions*, pavilions, tents.

" Ye lie, ye lie, ye liar loud !
   Sae loud I hear ye lie :
For Percy had not men yestreen
   To dight my men and me.

" But I have dream'd a dreary dream,
   Beyond the Isle of Sky ;
I saw a dead man win a fight,
   And I think that man was I."

He belted on his guid braid sword,
   And to the field he ran ;
But he forgot the helmet good,
   That should have kept his brain.

When Percy wi' the Douglas met,
   I wat he was fu' fain ;
They swakked their swords, till sair they swat,
   And the blood ran down like rain.

But Percy with his guid braid sword,
   That could so sharply wound,
Has wounded Douglas on the brow,
   Till he fell to the ground.

Then he called on his little foot-page,
   And said—" Run speedily,
And fetch my ain dear sister's son,
   Sir Hugh Montgomery.

swakked, smote.

"My nephew good," the Douglas said,
 "What recks the death of ane !
Last night I dream'd a dreary dream,
 And I ken the day's thy ain.

"My wound is deep ; I fain would sleep ;
 Take thou the vanguard of the three,
And hide me by the bracken bush,
 That grows on yonder lily lea.

"O bury me by the bracken bush,
 Beneath the blooming briar,
Let never living mortal ken
 That ere a kindly Scot lies here."

He lifted up that noble lord,
 Wi' the saut tear in his ee ;
He hid him in the bracken bush,
 That his merry-men might not see.

The moon was clear, the day drew near,
 The spears in flinders flew,
But mony a gallant Englishman
 Ere day the Scotsmen slew.

The Gordons good, in English blood
 They steeped their hose and shoon ;
The Lindsays flew like fire about,
 Till all the fray was done.

flinders, fragments.

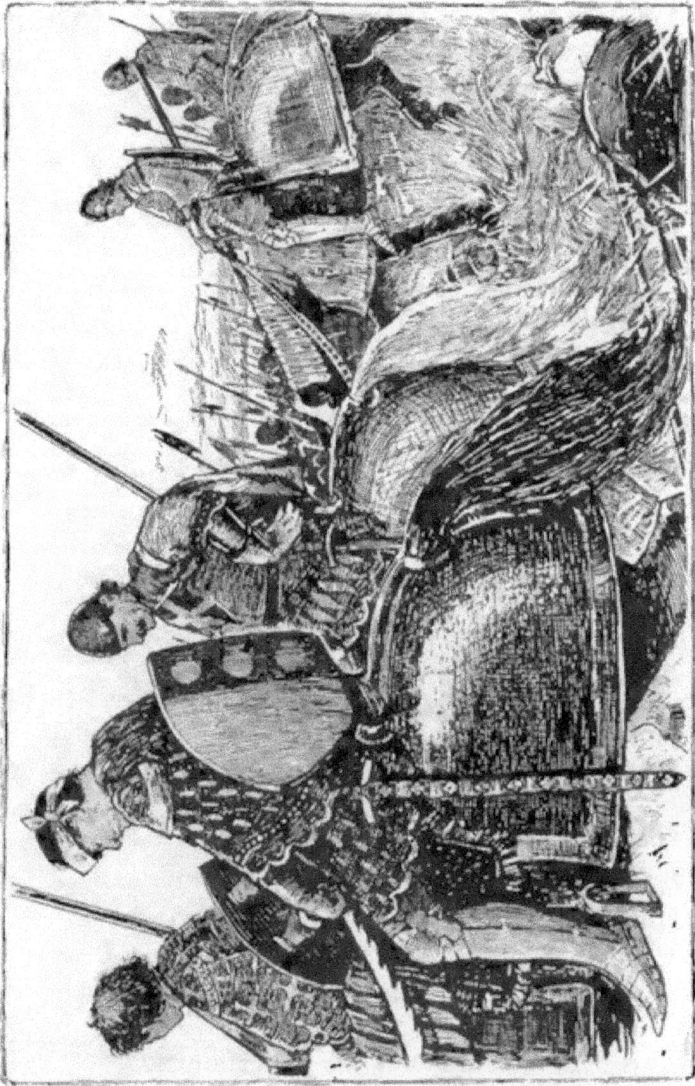

The Percy and Montgomery met,
  That either of other were fain ;
They swapped swords, and they twa swat,
  And aye the blood ran down between.

" Now yield thee, yield thee, Percy," he said,
  " Or else I vow I'll lay thee low ! "
" To whom must I yield," quoth Earl Percy,
  " Now that I see it must be so ? "

" Thou shalt not yield to lord nor loon,
  Nor yet shalt thou yield to me ;
But yield thee to the bracken bush,
  That grows upon yon lily lea."

" I will not yield to a bracken bush,
  Nor yet will I yield to a briar ;
But I would yield to Earl Douglas,
  Or Sir Hugh the Montgomery, if he were
    here."

As soon as he knew it was Montgomery,
  He struck his sword's point in the ground ;
The Montgomery was a courteous knight,
  And quickly took him by the hand.

This deed was done at the Otterbourne,
  About the breaking of the day ;
Earl Douglas was buried at the bracken bush
  And the Percy led captive away.

swapped, smote.

≈ The Bonny Lass
of Anglesey ≈

Our king he has a secret to tell,
    And ay well keepit it must be ;
The English lords are coming down
    To dance and win the victory.

Our king has cried a noble cry,
    And ay well keepit it must be :
" Gar saddle ye, and bring to me
    The bonny lass of Anglesey."

Up she starts, as white as the milk,
    Between him and his company :
" What is the thing I hae to ask,
    If I should win the victory ? "

" Fifteen ploughs but and a mill
    I gie thee till the day thou die,
And the fairest knight in a' my court
    To chuse thy husband for to be."

She's taen the fifteen lord[s] by the hand,
    Saying, " Will ye come dance with me ? "
But on the morn at ten o'clock
    They gave it o'er most shamefully.

Up then raise the fifteenth lord—
    I wat an angry man was he—
Laid by frae him his belt and sword,
    And to the floor gaed manfully.

He said, "My feet shall be my dead
    Before she win the victory;"
But before't was ten o'clock at night
    He gaed it o'er as shamefully.

⇜ The Wee
⇜ Wee Man

As I was walking all alone,
    Atween a water and a wa',
And there I spied a wee wee man,
    He was the least that ere I saw.

His legs were scarce a shathmont's length,
    And thick and thimber was his thigh;
Between his brows there was a span,
    And between his shoulders there was three.

He took up a mickle stane,
    And he flang't as far as I could see;
Though I had been a Wallace wight,
    I couldna liften't to my knee.

shathmont, six inches.

"O wee wee man, but thou be strang!
  Oh, tell me where thy dwelling be?"
"My dwelling's down at yon bonnie bower,
  O will ye go with me and see?"

On we lap, and awa' we rade,
  Till we came to yon bonny green;
We lighted down for to bait our horse,
  And out there cam a lady fine;

Four and twenty at her back,
  And they were a' clad out in green;
Though the King of Scotland had been there,
  The warst o' them might hae been his queen.

On we lap, and awa' we rade,
  Till we came to yon bonny ha';
Where the roof was o' the beaten gowd,
  And the floor was o' the crystal a'.

When we cam to the stair foot
  Ladies were dancing, jimp and sma';
But in the twinkling of an eye,
  My wee wee man was clean awa.

lap, leapt.   *jimp*, slender.

Clerk Colvill,   ≋

≋   or the Mermaid

CLERK COLVILL and his lusty dame
  Were walking in the garden green ;
The belt around her stately waist
  Cost Clerk Colvill of pounds fifteen.

" O promise me now, Clerk Colvill,
  Or it will cost ye muckle strife,
Ride never by the wells of Slane,
  If ye wad live and brook your life."

" Now speak nae mair, my lusty dame,
  Now speak nae mair of that to me :
Did I ne'er see a fair woman,
  But I wad sin with her body ? "

He's ta'en leave o' his gay lady,
  Nought minding what his lady said,
And he's rode by the wells of Slane,
  Where washing was a bonny maid.

" Wash on, wash on, my bonny maid,
  That wash sae clean your sark of silk ; "
" And weel fa' you, fair gentleman,
  Your body whiter than the milk."

brook, preserve.   sark, skirt.

. . . .

Then loud, loud cried the Clerk Colvill,
 "O my head it pains me sair ; "
" Then take, then take," the maiden said,
 " And frae my sark you'll cut a gare."

Then she's gi'ed him a little bane-knife,
 And frae her sark he cut a share ;
She's tied it round his whey-white face,
 But ay his head it ached mair.

Then louder cried the Clerk Colvill,
 " O sairer, sairer aches my head ; "
" And sairer, sairer ever will,"
 The maiden cries, " till you be dead."

Out then he drew his shining blade,
 Thinking to stick her where she stood ;
But she was vanish'd to a fish,
 And swam far off, a fair mermaid.

" O mother, mother, braid my hair ;
 My lusty lady, make my bed ;
O brother, take my sword and spear,
 For I have seen the false mermaid."

. . . .

gare, gore.   *bane*, bone.

Lady Isabel and ≈
≈ the Elf-Knight

FAIR lady Isabel sits in her bower sewing,
  Aye as the gowans grow gay;
There she heard an elf-knight blawing his horn,
  The first morning in May.

" If I had yon horn that I hear blawing,
And yon elf-knight to sleep in my bosom."

This maiden had scarcely these words spoken,
Till in at her window the elf-knight has luppen.

" It's a very strange matter, fair maiden," said he,
" I canna blaw my horn, but ye call on me."

" But will ye go to yon greenwood side,
If ye canna' gang, I will cause you to ride."

He leapt on a horse, and she on another,
And they rode on to the greenwood together.

" Light down, light down, lady Isabel," said he,
" We are come to the place where ye are to die."

" Hae mercy, hae mercy, kind sir, on me,
Till ance my dear father and mother I see."

gowans, flowers.

"Seven king's-daughters here hae I slain,
And ye shall be the eight o' them."

"O sit down a while lay your head on my knee,
That we may hae some rest before that I die."

She strok'd him sae fast, the nearer he did creep,
Wi' a sma' charm she lull'd him fast asleep.

Wi' his ain sword belt sae fast as she ban' him,
With his ain dag-dirk sae sair as she dang him.

"If seven kings' daughters here ye ha'e slain,
Lie ye here, a husband to them a'."

—•≔∣≖•—

∾ Fair Janet ∾

"YE maun gang to your father, Janet,
    Ye maun gang to him soon ;
Ye maun gang to your father, Janet,
    In case that his days are dune!"

Janet's awa' to her father,
    As fast as she could hie ;
"O what's your will wi' me, father?
    O what's your will wi' me?"

ban', bound.   *dag-dirk*, dagger.   *dang*, struck.

"My will wi' you, Fair Janet," he said,
  "It is both bed and board;
Some say that ye lo'e Sweet Willie,
  But ye maun wed a French lord."

"A French lord maun I wed, father?
  A French lord maun I wed?
Then, by my sooth," quo' Fair Janet,
  "He's ne'er enter my bed."

Janet's awa' to her chamber,
  As fast as she could go;
Wha's the first ane that tapped there,
  But Sweet Willie her jo!

"O we maun part this love, Willie,
  That has been lang between;
There's a French lord coming o'er the sea
  To wed me wi' a ring;
There's a French lord coming o'er the sea,
  To wed and tak me hame."

"If we maun part this love, Janet,
  It causeth mickle woe;
If we maun part this love, Janet,
  It makes me into mourning go."

"But ye maun gang to your three sisters,
  Meg, Marion, and Jean;
Tell them to come to Fair Janet,
  In case that her days are dune."

Willie's awa to his three sisters,
　　Meg, Marion, and Jean ;
"O haste, and gang to Fair Janet,
　　I fear that her days are dune."

Some drew to them their silken hose,
　　Some drew to them their shoon,
Some drew to them their silk mantles,
　　Their coverings to put on ;
And they're awa' to Fair Janet,
　　By the high light o' the moon.

　　．　　．　　．　　．　　．　　．　　．

"O I have born this babe, Willie,
　　Wi' mickle toil and pain ;
Take hame, take hame, your babe, Willie,
　　For nurse I dare be nane."

He's tane his young son in his arms,
　　And kissed him cheek and chin,—
And he's awa' to his mother's bower,
　　By the high light o' the moon.

"O open, open, mother," he says,
　　"O open, and let me in ;
The rain rains on my yellow hair,
　　And the dew drops o'er my chin,—
And I hae my young son in my arms,
　　I fear that his days are dune."

With her fingers lang and sma'
    She lifted up the pin ;
And with her arms lang and sma'
    Received the baby in.

" Gae back, gae back now, Sweet Willie,
    And comfort your fair lady ;
For where ye had but ae nourice,
    Your young son shall hae three."

Willie he was scarce awa',
    And the lady put to bed,
When in and came her father dear :
    " Make haste, and busk the bride."

" There's a sair pain in my head, father,
    There's a sair pain in my side ;
And ill, O ill, am I, father,
    This day for to be a bride.

" O ye maun busk this bonny bride,
    And put a gay mantle on ;
For she shall wed this auld French lord,
    Gin she should die the morn."

Some put on the gay green robes,
    And some put on the brown ;
But Janet put on the scarlet robes,
    To shine foremost through the town.

busk, dress.

And some they mounted the black steed,
　And some mounted the brown ;
But Janet mounted the milk-white steed,
　To ride foremost through the town.

" O wha will guide your horse, Janet ?
　O wha will guide him best ? "
" O wha but Willie, my true love,
　He kens I lo'e him best ! "

And when they cam to Mary's kirk,
　To tie the haly ban,
Fair Janet's cheek looked pale and wan,
　And her colour ga'ed and cam.

When dinner it was past and done,
　And dancing to begin,
" O we'll go take the bride's maidens,
　And we'll go fill the ring."

O ben then cam the auld French lord,
　Saying, " Bride, will ye dance with me ? "
" Awa', awa', ye auld French Lord.
　Your face I downa see."

O ben then cam now Sweet Willie,
　He cam with ane advance :
" O I'll go tak the bride's maidens,
　And we'll go tak a dance."

　　　　　downa, cannot.

" I've seen ither days wi' you, Willie,
    And so has mony mae ;
Ye would hae danced wi' me mysel',
    Let a' my maidens gae."

O ben then cam now Sweet Willie,
    Saying, " Bride, will ye dance wi' me ? "
" Aye, by my sooth, and that I will,
    Gin my back should break in three."

[And she's taen Willie by the hand,
    The tear blinded her e'e ;
" O I wad dance wi' my true love,
    Tho' bursts my heart in three ! "]

She hadna turned her through the dance,
    Through the dance but thrice,
Whan she fell doun at Willie's feet,
    And up did never rise !

[She's ta'en her bracelet frae her arm,
    Her garter frae her knee :
" Gie that, gie that, to my young son ;
    He'll ne'er his mother see."]

Willie's ta'en the key of his coffer,
    And gi'en it to his man ;
" Gae hame, and tell my mother dear,
    My horse he has me slain ;
Bid her be kind to my young son,
    For father he has nane."

["Gar deal, gar deal the bread," he cried,
　"Gar deal, gar deal the wine ;
This day has seen my true love's death,
　This night shall witness mine."]

The tane was buried in Mary's kirk,
　And the tither in Mary's quire :
Out of the tane there grew a birk,
　And the tither a bonny briar.

tane, one.　　　*tither*, other.

≈ Fair Helen ≈

PART SECOND.

I WISH I were where Helen lies,
Night and day on me she cries ;
O that I were where Helen lies,
    On fair Kirconnell Lee !

Curst be the heart that thought the thought,
And curst the hand that fired the shot,
When in my arms burd Helen dropt,
    And died to succour me !

O think na ye my heart was sair,
When my love dropt down and spak nae mair,
There did she swoon wi' mickle care,
    On fair Kirconnell Lee.

As I went down the water side,
None but my foe to be my guide,
None but my foe to be my guide,
    On fair Kirconnell Lee ;

I lighted down my sword to draw,
I hacked him in pieces sma',
I hacked him in pieces sma',
    For her sake that died for me.

    burd, maid.

O Helen fair, beyond compare!
I'll make a garland of thy hair,
Shall bind my heart for evermair,
    Until the day I die.

O that I were where Helen lies!
Night and day on me she cries;
Out of my bed she bids me rise,
    Says, " Haste and come to me! "—

O Helen fair! O Helen chaste!
If I were with thee, I were blest,
Where thou lies low, and takes thy rest,
    On fair Kirconnell Lee.

I wish my grave were growing green,
A winding-sheet drawn ower my een,
And I in Helen's arms lying,
    On fair Kirconnell Lee.

I wish I were where Helen lies!
Night and day on me she cries;
And I am weary of the skies,
    For her sake that died for me.

The

Cruel

Brother

THERE was three ladies play'd at the ba',
With a heigh-ho! and a lily gay;
There came a knight, and play'd o'er them a',
As the primrose spreads so sweetly.

The eldest was baith tall and fair,
But the youngest was beyond compare.

The midmost had a gracefu' mien,
But the youngest look'd like beauty's queen.

The knight bow'd low to a' the three,
But to the youngest he bent his knee.

The lady turned her head aside,
The knight he woo'd her to be his bride.

The lady blush'd a rosy red,
And said, " Sir knight, I'm too young to wed."

" O lady fair, give me your hand,
And I'll mak you lady of a' my land."

"Sir knight, ere you my favour win,
Ye maun get consent frae a' my kin."

He has got consent frae her parents dear,
And likewise frae her sisters fair.

He has got consent frae her kin each one,
But forgot to speir at her brother John.

Now, when the wedding day was come,
The knight would take his bonny bride home,

And many a lord and many a knight,
Came to behold that lady bright.

And there was nae man that did her see,
But wished himself bridegroom to be.

Her father dear led her down the stair,
And her sisters twain they kiss'd her there.

Her mother dear led her through the close,
And her brother John set her on her horse.

She lean'd her o'er the saddle-bow,
To give him a kiss ere she did go.

He has ta'en a knife, baith lang and sharp,
And stabb'd that bonny bride to the heart.

speir, ask.

She hadna ridden half thro' the town,
Until her heart's blood stained her gown.

" Ride saftly on," said the best young man,
" For I think our bonny bride looks pale and wan."

" O lead me gently up yon hill,
And I'll there sit down, and make my will."

" O what will you leave to your father dear ? "
" The silver-shod steed that brought me here."

" What will you leave to your mother dear ? "
" My velvet pall and silken gear."

" And what will you leave to your sister Ann ? "
" My silken scarf, and my gowden fan."

" What will ye leave to your sister Grace ? "
" My bloody clothes to wash and dress."

" What will ye leave to your brother John ? "
" The gallows-tree to hang him on."

" What will ye leave to your brother John's wife?"
" The wilderness to end her life."

This fair lady in her grave was laid,
And a mass was o'er her said.

But it would have made your heart right sair,
To see the bridegroom rive his hair.

rive, tear.

O

Lamkin

IT's Lamkin was a mason good
    As ever built with stane,
He built Lord Wearie's castle,
    But payment gat he nane.

"O pay me, Lord Wearie ;
    Come pay me my fee."
"I canna pay you Lamkin,
    For I maun gang o'er the sea."

"O pay me now, Lord Wearie ;
    Come, pay me out o' hand."
"I canna pay you, Lamkin,
    Unless I sell my land."

"O gin ye winna pay me,
    I here sall mak a vow,
Before that ye come hame again,
    Ye sall ha'e cause to rue."

Lord Wearie got a bonny ship,
    To sail the saut sea faem ;
Bade his lady weel the castle keep,
    Ay till he should come hame.

            faem, foam.

But the nourice was a fause limmer
    As e'er hung on a tree ;
She laid a plot wi' Lamkin,
    When her lord was o'er the sea.

She laid a plot wi' Lamkin,
    When the servants were awa' ;
Let him in at a little shot window,
    And brought him to the ha'.

" O where's a' the men o' this house,
    That ca' me Lamkin ? "
" They're at the barn well thrashing,
    'Twill be lang ere they come in."

" And where's the women o' this house,
    That ca' me Lamkin ? "
" They're at the far well washing ;
    'Twill be lang ere they come in."

" And where's the bairns o' this house,
    That ca' me Lamkin ? "
" They're at the school reading ;
    'Twill be night or they come hame."

" O where's the lady o' this house,
    That ca's me Lamkin ? "
" She's up in her bower sewing,
    But we soon can bring her down."

nourice, nurse. *limmer*, wretch. *shot-window*, projecting window.

Then Lamkin's tane a sharp knife,
    That hang down by his gair,
And he has gi'en the bonny babe
    A deep wound and a sair.

Then Lamkin he rocked,
    And the fause nourice sang,
'Till frae ilka bore o' the cradle
    The red blood out sprang.

Then out it spak the lady,
    As she stood on the stair,
" What ails my bairn, nourice,
    That he's greeting sae sair ?

" O still my bairn, nourice ;
    O still him wi' the pap ! "
" He winna still, lady,
    For this, nor for that."

" O still my bairn, nourice ;
    O still him wi' the wand ! "
" He winna still, lady,
    For a' his father's land."

" O still my bairn, nourice,
    O still him wi' the bell ! "
" He winna still, lady,
    Till ye come down yoursel'."

gair, skirt.   *bore*, hole.   *greeting*, crying.

O the firsten step she steppit,
   She steppit on a stane;
But the neisten step she steppit,
   She met him, Lamkin.

"O mercy, mercy, Lamkin!
   Ha'e mercy upon me!
Though you've ta'en my young son's life,
   Ye may let mysel' be."

"O sall I kill her, nourice?
   Or sall I lat her be?"
"O kill her, kill her, Lamkin,
   For she ne'er was good to me."

"O scour the basin, nourice,
   And mak it fair and clean,
For to keep this lady's heart's blood,
   For she's come o' noble kin."

"There need nae basin, Lamkin;
   Let it run through the floor;
What better is the heart's blood
   O' the rich than o' the poor?"

But ere three months were at an end,
   Lord Wearie came again;
But dowie dowie was his heart
   When first he came hame.

dowie, gloomy.

"O wha's blood is this," he says,
    " 'That lies in the châmer ?"
" It is your lady's heart's blood ;
    'Tis as clear as the lamer."

" And wha's blood is this," he says,
    " 'That lies in my ha' ?"
" It is your young son's heart's blood ;
    'Tis the clearest ava'."

O sweetly sang the black-bird
    That sat upon the tree ;
But sairer grat Lamkin,
    When he was condemn'd to die.

And bonny sang the mavis
    Out o' the thorny brake ;
But sairer grat the nourice,
    When she was tied to the stake.

≈ Cospatrick ≈

Cospatrick has sent o'er the faem ;
Cospatrick brought his lady hame ;
And fourscore ships have come her wi',
The lady by the green-wood tree.

lamer, amber.   *faem*, sea.

There were twal' and twal' wi' baken bread,
And twal' and twal' wi' gowd sae red,
And twal' and twal' wi' bouted flour,
And twal' and twal' wi' the paramour.

Sweet Willy was a widow's son,
And at her stirrup he did run ;
And she was clad in the finest pall,
But aye she let the tears down fall.

" O is your saddle set awry ?
Or rides your steed for you ower high ?
Or are you mourning, in your tide,
That you should be Cospatrick's bride ? "

" I am not mourning, at this tide,
That I should be Cospatrick's bride ;
But I am sorrowing in my mood,
That I should leave my mother good.

" But, gentle boy, come tell to me,
What is the custom of thy country ? "—
" The custom thereof, my dame," he says,
" Will ill a gentle lady please.

" Seven king's daughters has our lord wedded,
And seven king's daughters has our lord
    bedded ;
But he's cutted their breasts frae their breast-
    bane,
And sent them mourning hame again.

twal', twelve.   *bouted*, bolted.   *tide*, time.

" Yet, gin you're sure that you're a maid,
Ye may gae safely to his bed ;
But gif o' that ye be na sure,
Then hire some damsel o' your bower."—

The lady's call'd her bour maiden,
That waiting was into her train ;
" Five thousands merks I'll gie to thee,
To sleep this night with my lord for me."—

When bells were rung, and mass was sayen,
And a' men unto bed were gane,
Cospatrick and the bonny maid,
Into a chamber they were laid.

" Now, speak to me, blankets, and speak to
    me, bed,
And speak, thou sheet, enchanted web ;
And speak up, my bonny brown sword, that
    winna lie,
Is this a true maiden that lies by me ? "—

" It is not a maid that you hae wedded,
But it is a maid that you hae bedded ;
It is a leal maiden that lies by thee,
But not the maiden that it should be."—

O wrathfully he left the bed,
Aud wrathfully his claes on did ;
And he has ta'en him through the ha',
And on his mother he did ca'.

"I am the most unhappy man,
That ever was in Christian land!
I courted a maiden, meek and mild,
And I hae gotten naething but a woman wi'
    child."—

"O stay, my son, into this ha',
And sport ye wi' your merrymen a';
And I will to the secret bower,
To see how it fares wi' your paramour."—

The carline she was stark and sture,
She aff the hinges dang the dure;
"O is your bairn to laird or loon,
Or is it to your father's groom?"—

"O hear me, mother, on my knee,
Till my sad story I tell to thee:
O we were sisters, sisters seven,
We were the fairest under heaven.

"It fell on a summer's afternoon,
When a' our toilsome task was done,
We cast the kevils us amang,
To see which should to the green-wood gang.

"Ohon! alas, for I was youngest,
And aye my weird it was the hardest!
The kevil it on me did fa',
Whilk was the cause of a' my woe.

carline, old woman.   stark, strong.   sture, big.
dang, struck.   dure, door.   kevils, lots.   weird, destiny.

" For to the green-wood I maun gae,
To pu' the red rose and the slae ;
To pu' the red rose and the thyme,
To deck my mother's bower and mine.

"I hadna pu'd a flower but ane,
When by there came a gallant hend,
Wi' high-coll'd hose and laigh-coll'd shoon,
And he seem'd to be some king's son.

" And be I a maid, or be I nae,
He kept me there till the close o' day ;
And be I a maid, or be I nane,
He kept me there till the day was done.

" He gae me a lock o' his yellow hair,
And bade me keep it ever mair ;
He gae me a carknet o' bonny beads,
And bade me keep it against my needs.

" He gae to me a gay gold ring,
And bade me keep it abune a' thing."—
" What did ye wi' the tokens rare,
That ye gat frae that gallant there ?"—

" O bring that coffer unto me,
And a' the tokens ye sall see."—
" Now stay, daughter, your bower within,
While I gae parley wi' my son."—

slae, sloe.   hend, handsome.   coll'd, cut.   laigh, low.
carknet, necklace.

O she has ta'en her thro' the ha,
And on her son began to ca';
" What did ye wi' the bonny beads
I bade you keep against your needs?

" What did you wi' the gay gold ring
I bade you keep abune a' thing ? "—
" I gae them to a lady gay,
I met on green-wood on a day.

" But I wad gie a' my halls and towers,
I had that lady within my bowers ;
But I wad gie my very life,
I had that lady to my wife."—

" Now keep, my son, your halls and towers,
Ye have the bright burd in your bowers ;
And keep, my son, your very life,
Ye have that lady to your wife."—

Now, or a month was come and gane,
The lady bare a bonny son ;
And 'twas weel written on his breast-bane,
" Cospatrick is my father's name."
" O row my lady in satin and silk,
And wash my son in the morning milk."

burd, maid.   *row*, wrap.

Young Tam Lin.

" O I forbid ye, maidens a',
   That wear gowd on your hair,
To come or gae by Carterhaugh,
   For young Tam Lin is there.

" There's nane that gaes by Carterhaugh,
   But they leave him a wad,
Either their rings, or green mantles,
   Or else their maidenhead.

Janet has kilted her green kirtle,
   A little aboon her knee ;
And she has braided her yellow hair,
   A little aboon her bree,
And she's awa to Carterhaugh,
   As fast as she can hie.

wad, wager, forfeit.   *bree*, brow.

When she came to Carterhaugh,
  Tam Lin was at the well ;
And there she found his steed standing,
  But away was himsel'.

She hadna pu'd a double rose,
  A rose but only twa ;
Till up then started Young Tam Lin,
  Says, " Lady, thou's pu' nae mae."

—" Why pu's thou the rose, Janet ?
  And why breaks thou the wand ?
Or why comes thou to Carterhaugh,
  Withouten my command ?"—

—" Carterhaugh it is my ain ;
   My daddy gave it me ;
I'll come and gang by Carterhaugh,
   And ask nae leave at thee."

Janet has kilted her green kirtle,
   A little aboon her knee ;
And she has snooded her yellow hair,
   A little aboon her bree,
And she is to her father's ha'
   As fast as she can hie.

Four and twenty ladies fair
   Were playing at the ba' ;
And out then came fair Janet,
   Ance the flower among them a'.

Four and twenty ladies fair
   Were playing at the chess ;
And out then came the fair Janet,
   As green as any grass.

Out then spak an auld gray knight,
   Lay o'er the castle wa',—
And says, " Alas ! fair Janet, for thee,
   But we'll be blamed a' ! "—

" Haud your tongue, ye auld faced knight !
   Some ill death may ye die ;
Father my bairn on whom I will,
   I'll father nane on thee."—

Out then spak her father dear,
    And he spak meek and mild—
" And ever, alas ! sweet Janet," he says,
    " I think thou gaes with child."—

" And if I gae with child, father,
    Mysel' maun bear the blame ;
There's ne'er a laird about your ha'
    Shall get the bairnie's name.

" If my love were an earthly knight,
    As he's an elfin grey,
I wadna gie my ain true love
    For nae lord that ye hae.—

" The steed that my true love rides on,
    Is lighter than the wind ;
Wi' siller he is shod before,
    Wi' burning gowd behind."

Janet has kilted her green kirtle,
  A little aboon her knee,
And she has snooded her yellow hair,
  A little aboon her bree.
And she's awa to Carterhaugh,
  As fast as she can hie.

And when she came to Carterhaugh,
  Tam Lin was at the well ;
And there she found his steed standing,
  But away was himsel'.

She hadna pu'd a double rose,
  A rose but only twa,
Till up then started young Tam Lin,
  Says—"Lady, thou pu's nae mae !

"Why pu' ye the rose, Janet,
  Amang the groves sae green,
And a' to kill the bonny babe,
  That we gat us between ?"

"O tell me, tell me, Tam Lin," she says,
  "For's sake that died on tree,
If e'er ye was in holy chapel,
  Or christendom did see?"—

["The truth I'll tell to thee, Janet,
  A word I winna lie;
A knight me got, and a lady me bore,
  As well as they did thee.]

"Roxburgh, he was my grandfather,
  Took me with him to bide,
And ance it fell upon a day
  That wae did me betide.

And ance it fell upon a day,
  A cauld day and a snell,
That we were frae the hunting come,
  That frae my horse I fell;
The Queen of Fairies she caught me,
  In yon green hill to dwell;

"And pleasant is the fairy land, Janet,
  But, an eerie tale to tell,
Aye, at the end of seven years,
  We pay a teind to hell;
And I am sae fair and fu o' flesh,
  I fear 'twill be mysel'.

snell, keen.   *teind*, tithe.

P

" But the night is Hallowe'en, lady,
    The morn is Hallowday ;
Then win me, win me, an ye will,
    For well I wot ye may.

" Just at the mirk and midnight hour
    The fairy folk will ride ;
And they that wad their true-love win,
    At Miles Cross they maun bide."

" But how shall I thee ken, Tam Lin ?
    Or how my true love knaw,
Amang so many unco knights,
    The like I never saw ? "

" O first let pass the black, lady,
    And syne let pass the brown ;
But quickly run to the milk-white steed,
    Pu' ye his rider down.

" For I'll ride on the milk-white steed,
    And ay nearest the town ;
Because I was an earthly knight,
    They gie me that renown.

" My right hand will be gloved, lady,
    My left hand will be bare ;
Cocked up shall my bonnet be,
    And kaimed down shall my hair,
And thae's the tokens I gie thee,
    Nae doubt I will be there.

unco, strange.

" They'll turn me in your arms, Janet,
   Into an esk and adder ;
But hold me fast, and fear me not,
   I am your bairn's father.

" They'll turn me to a bear sae grim,
   And then a lion bold ;
But hold me fast, and fear me not,
   As ye shall love your child.

" Again they'll turn me in your arms,
   To a red-hot gaud of airn ;
But haud me fast, and fear me not,
   I'll do to you nae harm.

" And last they'll turn me in your arms
   Into the burning gleed ;
Then throw me into will-water,
   O throw me in wi' speed.

" And then I'll be your ain true-love,
   I'll turn a naked knight ;
Then cover me wi' your green mantle,
   And cover me out o' sight."

Gloomy, gloomy, was the night,
   And eerie was the way,
As fair Jenny, in her green mantle,
   To Miles Cross she did gae.

esk, newt.   *gaud of airn*, bar of iron.   *gleed*, coal.

About the midle o' the night,
  She heard the bridles ring ;

This lady was as glad at that
  As any earthly thing.

First she let the black pass by,
　And syne she let the brown ;
But quickly she ran to the milk-white steed,
　And pu'd the rider down.

Sae weel she minded what he did say,
　And young Tam Lin did win ;
Syne covered him wi' her green mantle,
　As blithe's a bird in spring.

Out then spake the Queen o' Fairies,
　Out of a bush o' broom—
" Them that has gotten young Tam Lin,
　Has gotten a stately groom."—

Out then spake the Queen o' Fairies,
　And an angry women was she,
" Shame betide her ill-fared face,
　And an ill death may she die,
For she's ta'en awa' the bonniest knight
　In a' my company.

" But had I kenn'd, Tam Lin," she says,
　" What now this night I see,
I wad hae ta'en out thy twa grey een,
　Put in twa een o' tree."

tree, wood.

The
⪥ Broomfield Hill ⪤

THERE was a knight and a lady bright,
   Had a true tryst at the broom ;
The ane ga'ed early in the morning,
   The other in the afternoon.

And aye she sat in her mother's bower door,
   And aye she made her mane,
" O whether should I gang to the Broomfield
     hill,
   Or should I stay at hame ?

" For if I gang to the Broomfield hill,
   My maidenhead is gone ;
And if I chance to stay at hame,
   My love will ca' me mansworn."—

Up then spake a witch-woman,
   Ay from the room aboon ;
" O, ye may gang to Broomfield hill,
   And yet come maiden hame.

" For when ye come to the Broomfield hill,
   Ye'll find your love asleep,
With a silver belt about his head,
   And a broom-cow at his feet.

mansworn, perjured.   *broom-cow*, bush of broom.

" Take ye the blossom of the broom,
　The blossom it smells sweet,
And strew it at your true love's head,
　And likewise at his feet.

" Take ye the rings off your fingers,
　Put them on his right hand,
To let him know, when he doth awake,
　His love was at his command."—

She pu'd the broom flower on Hive-hill,
　And strew'd on's white hals-bane,
And that was to be wittering true,
　That maiden she had gane.

" O where were ye, my milk-white steed,
　That I hae coft sae dear,
That wadna watch and waken me,
　When there was maiden here ?"—

" I stamped wi' my foot, master,
　And gar'd my bridle ring ;
But nae kin' thing wad waken ye,
　Till she was past and gane."—

" And wae betide ye, my gay gosshawk,
　That I did love sae dear,
That wadna watch and waken me,
　When there was maiden here."—

hals, neck.　　　　　　wittering, witness.
coft, bought.　　gar'd, made.　　kin', kind of.

"I clapped wi' my wings, master,
  And aye my bells I rang,
And aye cry'd, Waken, waken, master,
  Before the lady gang."—

"But haste and haste, my gude white steed,
  To come the maiden till,
Or a' the birds of gude green wood
  Of your flesh shall have their fill."—

"Ye needna burst your gude white steed,
  Wi' racing o'er the howm ;
Nae bird flies faster through the wood,
  Than she fled through the broom."

❦ Young Johnstone ❦

YOUNG Johnstone and the young Col'nel
  Sat drinking at the wine :
"O gin ye wad marry my sister,
  It's I wad marry thine."

"I wadna marry your sister,
  For a' your houses and land ;
But I'll keep her for my leman,
  When I come o'er the strand.

howm, flats.

" I wadna marry your sister,   .
   For a' your gowd so gay ;
But I'll keep her for my leman,
   When I come by the way."

Young Johnstone had a little small sword,
   Hung low down by his gair,
And he stabbed it through the young Col'nel
   That word he ne'er spak mair.

But he's awa' to his sister's bower,
   He's tirled at the pin :
" Where hae ye been, my dear brither,
   Sae late a coming in ? "
" I hae been at the school, sister,
   Learning young clerks to sing."

" I've dreamed a dreary dream this night,
   I wish it may be for good ;
They were seeking you with hawks and
      hounds,
   And the young Col'nel was dead."

" Hawks and hounds they may seek me,
   As I trow well they be ;
For I have killed the young Col'nel,
   And thy own true love was he."

gair, skirt.

"If ye hae killed the young Col'nel,
    O dule and wae is me ;
But I wish ye may be hanged on a high gallows,
    And hae nae power to flee."

And he's awa' to his true love's bower,
    He's tirled at the pin :
"Where hae ye been, my dear Johnstone,
    Sae late a coming in ? "
"It's I hae been at the school," he says,
    "Learning young clerks to sing."

"I have dreamed a dreary dream," she says,
    "I wish it may be for good ;
They were seeking you with hawks and hounds,
    And the young Col'nel was dead."

"Hawks and hounds they may seek me,
    As I trow well they be ;
For I hae killed the young Col'nel,
    And thy ae brother was he."

"If ye hae killed the young Col'nel,
    O dule and wae is me ;
But I care the less for the young Col'nel,
    If thy ain body be free.

"Come in, come in, my dear Johnstone,
    Come in and take a sleep ;
And I will go to my casement,
    And carefully I will thee keep."

dule, sad.

He had not weel been in her **bower-door**,
  No not for half an hour,
When four-and-twenty belted knights
  Came riding to the bower.

" Well may you sit and see, Lady,
  Well may you sit and say ;
Did you not see a bloody squire
  Come riding by this way ? "

" What colour were his hawks ? " she says,
  " What colour were his hounds ?
What colour was the gallant steed
  That bore him from the bounds ! "

" Bloody, bloody were his hawks,
  And bloody were his hounds ;
But milk-white was the gallant steed
  That bore him from the bounds."

" Yes, bloody, bloody were his hawks,
  And bloody were his hounds ;
And milk-white was the gallant steed
  That bore him from the bounds.

" Light down, light down now, gentlemen,
  And take some bread and wine ;
An the steed be swift that he rides on,
  He's past the brig o' Lyne."

An, if.

"We thank you for your bread, fair Lady,
  We thank you for your wine ;
But I wad gie thrice three thousand pound,
  That bloody knight was ta'en."

"Lie still, lie still, my dear Johnstone,
  Lie still and take a sleep ;
For thy enemies are past and gone,   .
  And carefully I will thee keep."

But young Johnstone had a little wee sword,
  Hung low down by his gair,
And he stabbed it in fair Annet's breast,
  A deep wound and a sair.

"What aileth thee now, dear Johnstone ?
  What aileth thee at me ?
Hast thou not got my father's gold,
  But and my mither's fee ?"

"Now live, now live, my dear Lady,
  Now live but half an hour,
And there's no a leech in a' Scotland
  But what shall be in thy bower."

"How can I live, how shall I live ?
  Young Johnstone, do not you see
The red, red drops o' my bonny heart's blood
  Rin trinkling down my knee ?

trinkling, trickling.

" But take thy harp into thy hand,
    And harp out ower yon plain,
And ne'er think mair on thy true love
    Than if she had never been."

He hadna weel been out o' the stable,
    And on his saddle set,
Till four-and-twenty broad arrows
    Were thrilling in his heart.

⸺⸺≋-I-≋⸺

≋ Jock o'
the Side ≋

Now Liddesdale has ridden a raid,
    But I wot they had better stayed at hame ;
For Mitchell o' Winfield he is dead,
    And my son Johnnie is prisoner tane.
        With my fa ding diddle, la la low diddle.

For Mangerton-House Auld Downie is gane,
    Her coats she has kilted up to her knee ;
And down the water wi' speed she rins,
    While tears in spates fa' fast frae her eye.

spates, torrents.

Then up and bespake the Lord Mangerton,
  "What news, what news, sister Downie, to
    me ?"
" Bad news, bad news, my Lord Mangerton ;
  Mitchell is kill'd, and tane they hae my son
    Johnnie."

" Ne'er fear, sister Downie," quo' Mangerton ;
  " I hae yokes of oxen, four and twenty ;
My barns, my byres, and my faulds, a' weel fill'd,
  And I'll part wi' them a', ere Johnnie shall die.

" Three men I'll take to set him free,
  Weel harness'd a' wi' best o' steel ;
The English rogues may hear, and dree
  The weight o' their braid-swords to feel.

" The Laird's Jock ane, the Laird's Wat twa,
  O Hobie Noble, thou ane maun be ;
Thy coat is blue, thou hast been true,
  Since England banish'd thee, to me."

Now Hobie was an English man,
  In Bewcastle-dale was bred and born ;
But his misdeeds they were sae great,
  They banish'd him ne'er to return.

Lord Mangerton them orders gave,
  " Your horses the wrang way maun a' be shod ;
Like gentlemen ye must not seem,
  But look like corn-caugers gawn ae road.

byres, cow-houses.   *dree,* suffer.   *caugers,* carriers or dealers.

" Your armour gude ye maunna show,
  Nor ance appear like men o' weir ;
As country lads be all array'd,
  Wi' branks and brecham on ilk mare."

Sae now a' their horses are shod the wrang way,
  And Hobie has mounted his grey sae fine ;
Jock his lively bay, Wat's on his white horse
      behind,
  And on they rode for the water o' Tyne.

At the Choler-ford they a' light down,
  And there, wi' the help o' the light o' the
      moon,
A tree they cut, wi' fifteen nags upo' ilk side,
  To climb up the wa' o' Newcastle town.

But when they came to Newcastle town,
  And were alighted at the wa',
They found their tree three ells o'er laigh,
  They found their stick baith short and sma'.

Then up and spake the Laird's ain Jock,
  " There's naething for't, the gates we maun
      force ; "
But when they came the gates unto,
  A proud porter withstood baith men and
      horse.

weir, war.   branks, rope bridles.   brecham, collar.
tree, pole.   nags, notches.   laigh, low.

His neck in twa I wot they hae wrung,
  Wi' hand or foot he ne'er play'd paw ;
His life and his keys at ance they hae tane,
  And cast his body ahind the wa'.

Now soon they reach Newcastle jail,
  And to the pris'ner thus they call ;
"Sleeps thou, wakes thou, Jock o' the side,
  Or is thou wearied o' thy thrall ? "

Jock answers thus, wi' dolefu' tone—
  " Aft, aft I wake—I seldom sleep :
But wha's this kens my name sae weel,
  And thus to hear my waes does seek ? "

Then up spake the good Laird's Jock,
  " Ne'er fear ye now, my billy," quo' he ;
" For here's the Laird's Jock, the Laird's Wat,
  And Hobie Noble, come to set thee free."

" O hald thy tongue, and speak nae mair,
  And o' thy talk now let me be ;
For if a' Liddisdale were here the night,
  The morn's the day that I maun die.

" Full fifteen stane o' Spanish iron,
  They hae laid a' right sair on me ;
Wi' locks and keys I am fast bound
  Into this dungeon mirk and dreary."

          ne'er played paw, never stirred.

" Fear ye no that," quo' the Laird's Jock ;
  " A faint heart ne'er won a fair lady;
Work thou within, we'll work without,
  And I'll be bound we set thee free."

The first strong door that they came at,
  They loosed it without a key ;
The next chained door that they came at,
  They gar'd it a' in flinders flee.

The pris'ner now, upo' his back,
  The Laird's Jock's gotten up fu' high ;
And down the stair, him, irons and a',
  Wi' nae sma' speed and joy brings he.

" Now, Jock, I wot," quo' Hobie Noble,
  " Part o' the weight ye may lay on me ;"
" I wot weel no ! " quo' the Laird's Jock,
  " I count him lighter than a flea."

Sae out at the gates they a' are gane,
  The pris'ner's set on horseback high ;
And now wi' speed they've tane the gate,
  While ilk ane jokes fu' wantonly.

" O Jock, sae winsomely's ye ride,
  Wi' baith your feet upo' ae side !
Sae weel's ye're harness'd, and sae trig,
  In troth, ye sit like ony bride ! "

gar'd, made.   *flinders*, splinters.   *trig*, trim.

Q

The night, thou wot, they didna mind,
  But hied them on fu' merrily,
Until they came to Choler-ford brae,
  Where the water ran like mountains high.

But when they came to Choler-ford,
  There they met with an auld man ;
Says—" Honest man, will the water ride ?
  Tell us in haste, if that ye can."

" I wot weel no," quo' the good old man ;
  " Here I hae lived this thirty years and three,
And I ne'er yet saw the Tyne sae big,
  Nor rinnin' ance sae like a sea."

Then up and spake the Laird's saft Wat,
  The greatest coward in the company—
" Now halt, now halt, we needna try't ;
  The day is com'd we a' maun die ! "

" Poor faint-hearted thief ! " quo' the Laird's
    ain Jock,
  " There'll nae man die but he that's fie ;
I'll lead ye a' right safely through ;
  Lift ye the pris'ner on ahint me."

Sae now the water they a' hae tane,
  By anes and twas they a' swam through ;
" Here are we a' safe," says the Laird's Jock,
  " And, poor faint Wat, what think ye now ? "
    fie, predestined.

They scarce the ither side had won,
  When twenty men they saw pursue ;
Frae Newcastle town they had been sent,
  A' English lads, right good and true.

But when the land-sergeant the water saw,
  " It winna ride, my lads," quo' he ;
Then out he cries—" Ye the pris'ner may take,
  But leave the irons, I pray, to me."

" I wot weel no," cry'd the Laird's Jock,
  " I'll keep them a' ; shoon to my mare they'll
    be :
My good grey mare—for I am sure,
  She's bought them a' fu' dear frae thee."

Sae now they're away for Liddisdale,
  E'en as fast as they could them hie ;
The pris'ner's brought to his ain fire-side,
  And there o's airns they make him free.

" Now, Jock, my billy," quo' a' the three,
  " The day was com'd thou was to die ;
But thou's as weel at thy ain fire-side,
  Now sitting, I think, 'tween thee and me."

They hae gar'd fill up ae punch-bowl,
  And after it they maun hae anither,
And thus the night they a' hae spent,
  Just as they had been brither and brither.

airns, irons.

≈ There was a Maid
came out of Kent ≈

THERE was a maid came out of Kent,
    Dainty love, dainty love ;
There was a maid came out of Kent,
    Dangerous be :
There was a maid came out of Kent,
Fair, proper, small and gent,
As ever upon the ground went,
    For so it should be.

≈ The Fire of
Frendraught ≈

THE reek it rose, and the flame it flew,
    And oh the fire augmented high,
Until it came to Lord John's chamber-window
    And to the bed where Lord John lay.

"O help me, help me, Lady Frennet !
    I never ettled harm to thee ;
And if my father slew thy lord,
    Forget the deed and rescue me."

reek, smoke.   *ettled,* designed.

He looked east, he looked west,
 To see if any help was nigh ;
At length his little page he saw,
 Who to his lord aloud did cry.

" Loup down, loup down, my master dear !
 What though the window's dreigh and high ?
I'll catch you in my arms twa,
 And never a foot from you I'll flee."

" How can I loup, you little page,
 How can I leave this window high ?
Do you not see the blazing low,
 And my twa legs burnt to my knee ? "

  dreigh, high.   *low*, flame.

Robin
Hood's
Death
and
Burial

When Robin Hood and Little John,
    Down a down, a down, a down.
Went o'er yon bank of broom,
Said Robin Hood to Little John,
    "We have shot for many a pound :
      Hey down, a down, a down.

"But I am not able to shoot one shot more,
    My arrows will not flee ;
But I have a cousin lives down below,
    Please God, she will bleed me."

Now Robin is to fair Kirkley gone,
    As fast as he can win ;
But before he came there, as we do hear,
    He was taken very ill.

And when that he came to fair Kirkley-
    hall,
    He knock'd all at the ring,
But none was so ready as his cousin her-
    self
    For to let bold Robin in.

" Will you please to sit down, cousin Robin,"
        she said,
    " And drink some beer with me ? "
" No, I will neither eat nor drink,
    Till I am blooded by thee."

" Well, I have a room, cousin Robin," she
        said,
    " Which you did never see,
And if you please to walk therein,
    You blooded by me shall be."

She took him by the lily-white hand,
    And led him to a private room,
And there she blooded bold Robin Hood,
    Whilst one drop of blood would run.

She blooded him in the vein of the arm,
   And lock'd him up in the room ;
There did he bleed all the live-long day,
   Until the next day at noon.

He then bethought him of a casement door,
   Thinking for to be gone ;
He was so weak he could not leap,
   Nor he could not get down.

He then bethought him of his bugle-horn,
   Which hung low down to his knee ;
He set his horn unto his mouth,
   And blew out weak blasts three.

Then Little John, when hearing him,
   As he sat under the tree,
"I fear my master is near dead,
   He blows so wearily."

Then Little John to fair Kirkley is gone,
   As fast as he can dri'e ;
But when he came to Kirkley-hall,
   He broke locks two or three :

Until he came bold Robin to,
   Then he fell on his knee ;
"A boon, a boon," cries Little John,
   "Master, I beg of thee."

          dri'e, drive.

"What is that boon," quoth Robin Hood,
  "Little John, thou begs of me?"
"It is to burn fair Kirkley-hall,
  And all their nunnery."

"Now nay, now nay," quoth Robin Hood,
  "That boon I'll not grant thee;
I never hurt woman in all my life,
  Nor man in woman's company.

"I never hurt fair maid in all my time,
  Nor at my end shall it be;
But give me my bent bow in my hand,
  And a broad arrow I'll let flee;
And where this arrow is taken up,
  There shall my grave digg'd be.

"Lay me a green sod under my head,
  And another at my feet;
And lay my bent bow by my side,
  Which was my music sweet;
And make my grave of gravel and green,
  Which is most right and meet.

"Let me have length and breadth enough,
  With under my head a green sod;
That they may say, when I am dead,
  Here lies bold Robin Hood."

These words they readily promis'd him,
    Which did bold Robin please :
And there they buried bold Robin Hood,
    Near to the fair Kirklèys.

Index to Titles

VOL. I.

In this Index, as in Prof. Child's *English and Scottish Ballads*, the titles by which the ballads are designated in this volume have been printed in Roman letters; the alternative titles of these or other ballads referred to in the notes are printed in *Italics*.

www.ingramcontent.com/pod-product-compliance
Lightning Source LLC
Chambersburg PA
CBHW020505270326
41926CB00008B/753